'Jo Swinney knows what it means to be a nomad – to have a heart expanded from pursuit of a hundred horizons, yet feel heartsick for a patch of cultural and spiritual ground to call "mine". In *Home* she weaves a fabric of rich, poignant, and often hilarious stories that touch our own deep longing to belong, showing us along the way that contentment may be found in more places than we've imagined.

In Swinney I've found a favourite spiritual writer, and in *Home* I've found a book I will return to again and again. These are wonderfully grounding words for a restless, transient age.'

Sheridan Voysey, writer, speaker, broadcaster, and author

'This book is a rich, thought-provoking reflection on our sense of home. Drawing together personal story with biblical reflections we are taken on an inner journey which asks us to think about what home is for us, where we belong and who we really are. Highly recommended!'

Dr Paula R. Gooder, Bible Society Theologian in Residence

'If you've ever felt out of place, ever wondered where home is, ever found yourself longing for a home you've lost which no longer exists, this is a book that will both challenge and encourage you.

Jo Swinney's *Home* is a great read. It's a book that effortlessly weaves together biblical insights, bracing honesty and wisdom earned through life's challenges and

losses and somehow evinces strength wrapped in vulner-ability and infused by courage, all of which is underpinned by self-effacing laugh-out-loud humour. It's brilliant.'

Rev. Dr Calvin Samuel, London School of Theology

'The deep yearning for home lives in every single one of us. Whether it be the safe place where we can go as our undefended self without fear of being rejected or the whisper of a parent in our soul, we long for a place to be us. Jo Swinney's book interweaves the threads of her own story and the Bible's wisdom on the subject of home and in so doing creates a beautiful tapestry of hopefulness for us about what home might be. Jo reminds us that God has a place called home for each of us which is close to his heart and where we are finally and fully accepted for who we are. Her words evoke in us the whispered possibility that even the most lost of us can find a way home, because he has found a way to us.'

Rev. Malcolm Duncan, Gold Hill Baptist Church

'A heart-ache of a book, evoking and exploring our deepest human yearning to return, and to be, and to find our way home.'

Pete Greig, 24-7 Prayer

'Home is more than a roof over your head, as I discover every day working to find adoptive and foster homes for children in the care system. Reading Jo's graceful book will inspire us not only to appreciate something more of our own homes, but perhaps also help us to recognise the incredible privilege it is to offer others the home they so desperately need.'

Dr Krish Kandiah, Home for Good

'Anyone who has lived in five countries on three continents in twenty houses over thirty-eight years must have something to say about finding home. Jo Swinney weaves a book that is warm, witty and wise. Blending her story with others points a restless generation to where home really lies. Reading it did my heart good.'

Rev. Ian Coffey, author and speaker

'In *Home* Jo Swinney has given us a treasure. Incisive, honest and thought provoking she blows apart preconceptions and encourages us to think expansively, helping build a rich picture of what it means to belong. Whatever life stage you are at this book will provoke, inspire and comfort in equal measure, and ultimately help you discover what it is to be "at home".'

Katharine Hill, Care for the Family

'Jo's book is compassionate, compelling and relatable. Writing from a deeply personal perspective she speaks into the heart of what it means to be human.'

Rev. Kate Bottley, priest and *Gogglebox* star

'This is a really lovely gem of a book. Jo writes movingly and amusingly from her own experience and gives us not only a beautiful look at the longing that is in all our hearts

– for a place (and people) that we can call home – but the hope that to find such a thing is really possible.'

Dr Ruth Valerio, Tearfund

'A moving book – about moving home and more. Like Jo and so many of the people whose stories are told in this book, I had a peripatetic childhood, travelling around England and abroad. Around us, there seems to be no end to the streams of refugees, homeless people or those trapped in unhappy homes. For some, the search to find "home" is more troubled than others but we are all on that quest. Jo's beautifully written book, which draws on Scripture and other Christian teachings, is simply wonderful to have as a reflection and guide on the journey.'

Ruth Gledhill, Christian Today

HOME

The quest to belong

Jo Swinney

HODDER &
STOUGHTON

Unless indicated otherwise, Scripture quotations are taken from the
Holy Bible, New International Version (Anglicised edition). Copyright © 1979,
1984, 2011 by Biblica (formerly International Bible Society).
Used by permission. All rights reserved.

First published in Great Britain in 2017 by Hodder & Stoughton
An Hachette UK company

1

Copyright © Jo Swinney, 2017
Illustrations © Jo Swinney

A CIP catalogue record for this title is available from the British Library

ISBN 978 1 473 64865 4
eBook ISBN 978 1 473 64867 8

Printed and bound in the UK by Clays Ltd, St Ives plc

Hodder & Stoughton policy is to use papers that are natural, renewable and
recyclable products and made from wood grown in sustainable forests.
The logging and manufacturing processes are expected to conform to the
environmental regulations of the country of origin.

Hodder & Stoughton Ltd
Carmelite House
Victoria Embankment
London EC4Y 0DZ

www.hodderfaith.com

For Esther, Jeremy and Beth
O meu lar é onde vocês estão[1]

Contents

Setting out

The quest begins

MY NINE-YEAR-OLD DAUGHTER Alexa and I went for an autumn walk this morning, kicking through crunchy red and ochre leaves and walking carefully around puddles – one of us (not me) is too grown up to splash through them these days. We talked about this and that, and got around to the subject of a visit we're planning to our old neighbourhood, an hour's drive away. 'It still feels like home there,' she said. 'I know more people, and I like that it's quiet. I'm a village girl not a city girl. And it's where I've lived most of my life.' Numbers are not my strong suit, but I did a quick mental calculation, and she's right. She's lived here in Surbiton for less than half her years. I feel a little sad, and the ever-present parental guilt grows momentarily more acute. I wish she felt at home here. Alexa glances at me and, in her typically astute way, senses my reaction. 'I do feel at home here, Mummy,' she says, soothingly. 'Just not *as* at home as I did in our old house.'

I think about a conversation I had with a man seated next to me at a dinner recently. He told me that when he drove his son up to his own home town of Newcastle for university, leaving to come back down south felt like leaving home, even though he's lived in London for twenty-five years. I think about a friend who grew up in Pakistan and can't bear to think about it because the distance is too painful. I think about a woman I know who lived all her life in the same house but found it didn't feel like home any more when her beloved father died. So many of us carry, deep within us, a grief for the loss of somewhere we once belonged.

I've done a lot of thinking about home in my life, about where or who it is, about how I can create it wherever I am, or become it for those who need a safe place. I've wondered if the search for home is a fool's errand, a red herring of a quest, an illusion of gold at the foot of the rainbow. But I've persisted. I'm still a believer. And these days, most of the time, I feel at home. I wonder if you do?

Where is home? Our need for an answer to that question is profound. I came across the American psychologist Abraham Maslow at university in a course about poverty and development. He is best known for his 'hierarchy of needs' – a pyramid that moves from physiological needs at the base, up to safety, belonging, love, esteem, self-actualisation and finally self-transcendence.[1] His argument was that each layer of the pyramid is dependent on the layer below it. So many of these needs are met in the context of home.

In 1943 the philosopher, mystic and activist Simone Weil was asked by the French government in exile to come up with a plan for the restoration of a Europe devastated by war. Where would you begin with such a task? Absolutely everything from infrastructure to housing to food production to health care was in tatters. Simone began by considering basic human needs – some physical, but others needs of the soul. The soul's needs, she argued, were just as necessary to life as the body's. When they are not met, 'We fall little by little into a state more or less resembling death, more or less akin to a purely vegetative existence.' A state-of-the-art sewage system was all very well, but Europe's citizens were traumatised, and good sanitation alone wasn't going to heal a broken society.

What are the needs of the soul, then? Weil's concern was to identify the essential qualities of a society in which individuals could thrive. She was looking for the soul's equivalent to what food and warmth are to the body. For Europe to again become a place in which its citizens could flourish, there needed to be order, obedience, just punishment, security and equality. People would need freedom of opinion, the right to own property, and a common understanding of truth. All these are profound needs, and yet for Weil, 'To be rooted is perhaps the most important and least recognised need of the human soul.' We need to know where our home is.

We live in transient times. Those who live out their days in one place, and have no doubt whatsoever where they are from, are a dying breed. When I meet people like this, I bombard them with questions, trying to understand what it might be like to be them, to be identified so clearly with a particular location and community. Their experiences seem as exotic to me as my more nomadic history does to them. But my experience is more and more common. In 2015, 244 million people around the world lived outside their country of origin. In the UK in 2013 over a quarter of babies were born to mothers who were themselves born elsewhere. In London schools there are over 300 different languages spoken. We may choose to live abroad for study, marriage or adventure. Soldiers, missionaries, diplomats and oil-company employees relocate to far-flung lands for work. Or we may have no choice about leaving our home country. Countless people in this century alone have fled the effects of environmental disaster, war, persecution or an impossible economic situation.

Migration happens across borders but also within them. According to a survey carried out in 2012 by Bosch, makers of kitchen appliances, the average Brit moves house eight times during their life (thus requiring, Bosch no doubt hope, at least eight new fridges). Some of those moves will be relatively local – to larger properties in better areas of the same town, a move down the street to a smaller place when the kids move out, or to another rented property when a lease expires – but many take people to an entirely new context, where they must begin again. Who now has the luxury of restricting their job search to a familiar geographical radius? How many of us have family living close enough to help us out with regular childcare or to keep us company in old age? When we have moved to a location where we have no ties and no history, can it ever become more than a lodging place?

Literal homelessness is a massive issue, even in wealthy nations. Accurate figures are hard to obtain, as no one wants to assert their place on that particular slice of the pie chart, but walk through any city centre and you'll pass men and women who will bed down that night on the same doorsteps and paving slabs where they pass their days. And whatever the statistics, each individual case is a story of hardship and struggle. My husband Shawn lived in his car for several months through the harsh Minnesota winter when he turned eighteen; his mother would have lost housing benefit if he'd stayed with her, and he didn't have enough saved for a deposit on his own place. As a student I volunteered at a Salvation Army homeless drop-in centre, and I heard enough stories to know that the line between a settled and ordered life and destitution is more porous than anyone likes to think. In the UK, under the 1998 Housing Act, 'homelessness' means living somewhere without legal right of ownership or tenancy. This definition includes not only those sleeping rough on the street, but anyone who relies on the sofas of friends, hostels or squats. The lack of a place to call your own is destabilising and demoralising in the extreme.

﹍naps you have never experienced homelessness, or ﹍ved in a different culture. For you, home might take the form of people. You might have been thrown by how unsettled you were when your children grew up and moved away, or discovered that a relationship breakdown has left you feeling unsure of your place in the world. Where is home if you find you are alone?

There are many questions that will be raised in these pages: where do I belong, and who do I belong to? Is it okay for me to love my house, my furniture, books and paintings as much as I do? Is my sense of homesickness really a longing for the permanence of heaven and, if so, do I have to wait until I die to feel truly at home? How do I deal with the fact that my heart is in another country? How can I settle here when my loved ones are far away? Can this ever be my place when I only just got here and I don't know how long I can stay?

As well as questions, you will find stories here, some of mine and some that others have allowed me to share. I hope these stories will make you think about your own story, and that you'll tell your stories to others, and ask them theirs. It is in shaping and sharing our stories that we find answers to our deepest questions and face the fears that, while they lie buried deep, retain their power.

This seems a good moment to say that I'm a Christian. In the same way a secular humanist or a Muslim or a Buddhist or a Pastafarian (this is a thing – look it up if you don't believe me) writes from within their worldview, I write from within mine. Having said that, home is a subject that touches us all; I don't understand it to be an entirely spiritual concept upon which we'll struggle to find common ground if you don't share my faith. There's an oft-quoted line from Saint Augustine's account of his conversion, 'Confessions': 'Thou hast made us for thyself, O Lord, and our heart is restless until it finds its rest in thee.' Do I believe that ultimately we find the deepest, most unshakeable peace when we are in relationship with the Triune God of the Bible? Yes – and that shouldn't surprise you; like I said, I am a Christian. But I don't think that is the last word on feeling at home, and so I hope you'll stick with me and engage with the book and with me, even where we might see things differently. The same goes for my fellow Christians. I hold no illusions about the likelihood we will ever reach unity of thought on anything where more than one opinion is available, and I'm expecting and even hoping to spark some respectfully conducted debate.

I will also be retelling the David stories from 1 and 2 Samuel, perhaps with a bit of artistic licence thrown in here and there, but doing my best to stay close to the heart of what we know of David from the Bible. The wonderful thing about David is that as well as the historical third-person narrative, we also have the songs he wrote, his psalms – raw, personal God-ward thoughts and feelings that give the accounts of his life a whole other dimension. I've always felt a bit of a connection with David, not because I'm a hairy harpist with an affinity for sheep, but because I recognise David as a fellow wrestler with depression, as someone who loved God and yet made huge and horrible mistakes, as someone who sometimes felt rooted and secure and sometimes completely lost.

There are parts of David's life that are familiar even to those who have never read the Bible. Few have not heard of his face-off with the Philistine giant Goliath, or his adultery with the beautiful Bathsheba. But there is more to David's life than these respectively glorious and sordid episodes, and much we can learn from it about the meaning of home.

Sometimes we are tempted to approach biblical texts with the intention of extracting a comprehensive list of principles on a given topic. That is not the way God has chosen to communicate with us. Instead he has invested in developing relationships with people, flawed, fallible people, whose lives are shaped by him and who have in turn shaped history. The David stories won't give us a tidy theology of home, but they will give us a window into how the idea of home played out for 'a man after God's own heart'.

The American author David W. Henderson writes, 'Where do I land my anxious heart? Where do I take up residence and rest? Abide and abode are sister words. We rest in what we dwell in.' For a Christian, there is a sense in which God is our home – our security, our refuge, our place of unconditional belonging. However, in this exploration of home, my hope is that we won't be whittling away at definitions, trying to get to one, core essence of its meaning – which in a final Big Reveal is shown to be God, and God's place, heaven. Instead, picture us weaving a web, adding strand after strand until we have created something complex, beautiful and strong. Is home God? Yes, for me it is. But it is also a house. Is it God and a house? Yes, and it is a family and a community too. So it is all those things? Yes, and a country and a culture and a past and a settled acceptance of who I am, wherever I happen to be. You can take a thread from a spider's web and not destroy the structure. If we have a multi-faceted understanding of home, we won't become homeless (in a fundamental sense) if one of those facets is taken away. If we lose our house, if our marriage falls apart, if we have no job, if we are transplanted to another culture, we can still find home in the many other senses of the word.

I have had times when I have utterly despaired of ever feeling at home. Some of those times I've known where home was, but been unable to get there. At other times I've not known what it was or if it even existed. But I'm hopeful now. I'm hopeful for myself, and I'm hopeful for you.

Will you come on a journey with me – through my life, through David's, through yours? Let's head for home. I have a feeling we're going to find we don't have far to go.

CHAPTER ONE

Heart-sick

My home is not here

The crooked spire, Chesterfield

*Homesickness is not always a vague, nostalgic, almost
beautiful emotion, although that is somehow the way
we always seem to picture it in our mind. It can be a
terribly keen blade, not just a sickness in metaphor
but in fact as well.*

Stephen King, *The Body*

I LIKE TRAIN journeys. I like the way they give you a sense
of how you got to where you were going, the panoramic
views of field and sky, sudden slices of city innards and
the ugly beauty of industrial sidings. I like inventing
stories about my fellow passengers, and occasionally

making a surprising new friend. It's a good way to travel.

It was October, and I had a meeting to attend. I'd boarded my train in dirty London fog and three happy hours later walked out onto the sparkling station forecourt at Chesterfield. I'd booked a taxi to take me to Cliff College, twenty minutes away, and when it pulled up I recognised the driver. This was my third assignation with Gary, and his full facial tattoo no longer unnerved me. I hopped into the front seat, wondering if he remembered me as the slightly odd person who had asked him where taxi drivers go to the toilet.

I decided to start off on more conventional ground this time, and remarked on how much better the weather was here than in the Old Smoke. Turns out I'd hit a rich vein; Gary's favourite vein, in fact. For the next twenty minutes I was treated to a lyrical ode to Chesterfield.

Gary knows for sure he is the seventh generation to come from this mid-sized Derbyshire market town before the family history gets lost in the mists of time. I would say it is more than likely that in the first century his family helped build the Roman fort on the site of which Chesterfield grew up. He was born in a hospital two streets from his childhood home, which is two streets from his current address. 'Have you ever lived anywhere else?' I wanted to know. He swivelled his head and fixed me with a look of utter contempt. Why would he do such a thing? Just look at the place. I looked, and I confess the part of town we were passing through wasn't making his argument for him. He's the one who lives here, I thought, so it's good he can see the loveliness, even if it's passing me by.

Not only has Gary not lived anywhere else, he doesn't even like to leave it for a holiday. He'll go for a week, max, and then he has to come home. He gets homesick and miserable and begins to pine. The other day, he told me proudly, he gave a ride in his taxi to a lady who had come here on holiday.

We had left the town by now and were out in open country. I was able to tell him in all honesty that I could see the attraction – purple moorlands with dramatic rocky outcrops in the foreground, great sweeping hills meeting the sky on the horizon and a sense of space you don't find in many places on our crowded island.

'Look,' he said, reaching for his phone. I'd like to say he pulled over at this point. I'm a bit of a stickler for not driving and playing with phones – you know, the whole not-dying-in-a-car-accident hang-up. He wanted to show me pictures of Chesterfield's famous crooked spire. He had quite a collection. 'You really do love it, don't you?' I said, wonder in my voice. But Gary seemed to feel I hadn't quite grasped just how much he loves it, and he had more evidence. 'My wife put on Facebook the other day that she had got me to go shopping in Sheffield with her for the day. All my mates were posting comments like "Careful – he's going to get a nosebleed. He's not used to changing altitude!" and asking her what she'd had to do to get me to go with her.' I laughed, starting to think this was all a bit odd. But he was going on, and it was getting odder. 'You know when there were those riots in London?' I did. I also knew London was a fair distance from Chesterfield, as I'd had to sit on a train for nearly three hours to get from there to here. 'I was on holiday in Majorca – three days in. I told my wife we had to go home. I had to be there. I know it sounds weird, but I just felt like if the riots came to Chesterfield, I needed to be there to protect it.' And she understood this? 'The kids weren't happy, but we came home. The wife's from Chesterfield too,' he said. Of course she is.

I wanted to know if there were any downsides to living in Chesterfield. He gave it serious thought. It clearly isn't something he's been asked before. The taxi-drivers/toilet question was a first for him too; I can see myself becoming an anecdote for future customers. Finally he admitted it could be hard to misbehave when half the people you see doing your food shop in Asda, drink with in the pub, and carry around in your taxi have known you since you were an incontinent eight-pounder. It crossed my mind that this was a definite upside for his fellow Chesterfield residents, but then I realised I had drawn a specious connection between facial tattoos and crime, and repented of my prejudice.

As we arrived at the college, Gary said, 'So where are you from, then?' Good question. I didn't have time to give him the full story so I just said vaguely, 'Oh, all over really!' and waved him a cheery goodbye.

If Gary and I had had longer together, I would have told him something like this: I was born in Crawley, in the southeast of England. I don't remember it at all as I wasn't yet two when we moved to Bristol, so still in the south of England, but over to the west, for two years, where my sister Esther was born; and from there to Upton, Merseyside, in the north of England when I was three, where my brother Jeremy was born. From the ages of five to seventeen I lived in Portugal, where my parents established 'A Rocha', a Christian environmental conservation charity – and where my sister Beth was born. We moved four times during the first two and a half years, and then lived for nine years in an old farmhouse on a remote headland. When I was thirteen I went to boarding school in England, coming back to Portugal for holidays.

If Gary hadn't drifted off to sleep by this point, I would have then tried to explain how when I was seventeen my parents left Portugal and travelled the globe on behalf of the charity, leaving our family without a base for just under two years. Most of our possessions went into storage, our mail went to our grandparents' address, and we reconvened for school holidays in a variety of far-flung settings. Halfway through this period of unfixed abode I left boarding school and spent a year volunteering with an AIDS charity in Zimbabwe and travelling around South Africa, Mozambique, Malawi and Kenya, backpacker style. On my return to Europe, my parents had moved to a village in southern France, which was to be their home for the next fifteen years. Over the following three years I divided my time between there and Birmingham, where I was at university studying English literature and African studies. There was a house move in each place. After graduation I went to Vancouver, Canada, to study for a Masters in Theology at Regent College. I lived in Vancouver for four years in two different houses, and it was there that I met and married my American husband, Shawn. We moved together to Chalfont St Peter, just outside London, for a respectable nine years, with only one house move, and during this period our daughters, Alexa and Charis, were born. At time of writing we've been living in Surbiton for three years. For those of you who like numbers, that adds up to five countries, three continents and twenty houses (give or take) in thirty-eight years.

Where am I from? Everywhere and nowhere.

There were periods in history when societies and communities stayed put, as Gary's family has done. People were born by and large where their parents were born, and there they lived and gave birth to their own children. But now, so many of us have become drifters, tumbleweed blown by the winds of necessity and fancy. We move in then move on, sometimes just for a change of scene. And then, one day, we find ourselves standing wedged in between the buffet table and the door, juggling our glass of red wine and our saucer of quiche and crisps and trying to come up with a coherent answer to the offhand opener 'Where's home for you then?' without dissolving in tears. Because we suddenly realise we have no idea.

More than a metaphor

'Home' can be a complex and potentially painful concept, because it is not just an address. As Charles Dickens wrote, 'Home is a name, a word, it is a strong one; stronger than magician ever spoke, or spirit ever answered to, in the strongest conjuration.' The very word 'home' is hugely emotive. It might give us a warm feeling inside, something the Danes call *hygge* – which means a delightful combination of cosiness, safety, connection and happiness. A happy home is a source of security; it gives us a base from which to venture into the world with confidence. It is the places and the people where we are known and accepted, where we can be sure of a welcome. But we don't always get to return home, and not everyone has experienced safe places of belonging. The very word 'home' might catch us off guard and tip us into a downward spiral of longing that we fear may never be assuaged. There is something deep within all of us that knows a need for home, and when this need is not met, even temporarily, we feel pain. We get homesick.

I've had a lot of homes, and I've known a lot of homesickness. My suspicion is that I'm not alone. Pulitzer prizewinner John Cheever wrote, 'Fifty percent of the people in the world are homesick all the time . . . When you're in one place and long to be in another, it isn't as simple as taking a boat. You don't really long for another country. You long for something in yourself that you don't have, or haven't been able to find.' If he is anywhere near right, homesickness has reached epidemic proportions, and it has spread beyond those we'd perhaps most expect to be afflicted – the ten-year-old boy dispatched to boarding school, the university student away from home for the first time, the soldier on tour in the Middle East. I think a lot of us suffer from chronic low-grade homesickness, purely and simply because we are not quite sure where home is, but we do know we're not there.

Homesickness is not always a simple matter of missing a place. We can be homesick for a group of friends now dispersed, for a landscape altered by construction or climate, or for a period of time long gone when we felt settled. The newly retired can be hit by unexpected homesickness for their workplace or their role; a job loss under any circumstance can provoke a bout of homesickness. For Christians, expectant of a permanent, eternal home with God in heaven, homesickness can be about somewhere never seen and not yet experienced. Adults can be homesick for childhood, when they had people to look after them and no responsibilities. Children get homesick when their surroundings change, thrown by a rearrangement of the furniture or a new colour of paint on the front door. One of the nicest things Shawn has ever said to me is that when I'm away he's homesick for me.

Whatever the cause, if you've ever been homesick you'll know it's not pleasant. My first experience of homesickness was during the initial months of living in Portugal, and it wasn't particularly bad. My main symptoms were a craving for dolly mixtures and drumstick lollies and the occasional cry because I missed my best friend Joey Elliot and wasn't doing great at finding her replacement. At only five years old, I soon adapted to the new confectionery on offer and my memories of England became hazy.

Homesickness struck with force, though, during my first

term at boarding school in England when I was thirteen. I'd been so focused on how great it would be to leave my school in the Algarve – where I'd been the butt of cruel jokes for years – that I was totally unprepared. It was crippling, a great gravity-force longing in the pit of my stomach to be back with my family, in the house I loved, in the country that had become my country. I remember making a little window with my hands, framing a piece of sky, and trying to trick my mind into thinking I was looking at Algarvian sky on an unusually grey day. I knew to the minute just how long I had to wait until the school holidays.

Since that first year at boarding school I've experienced plenty more homesickness, some bouts only lasting as long as the smoke from a certain brand of cigarette hung in the air, and longer episodes of the kind that gnaws like hunger when you don't know where the next meal is coming from. I've woken from vivid dreams of places I've loved with tears drying on my cheeks, utterly heartbroken because I'm not there; and I've experienced an almost pleasant nostalgic ache for times gone by. There's a beautiful word in Portuguese for which we have no exact equivalent: *saudade*. It encompasses the idea of yearning, pining – a melancholic sense of something or someone missing. It is a gift of a word for those of us who have such feelings.

I wasn't homesick in Zimbabwe, or at university, or when I moved to Canada; but not because I'd grown strong and healthily self-reliant. It took an art project I did as part of my Masters to show me how I'd warped my understanding of home in order to protect myself from hurt.

Roots

Somewhere near the beginning of my Canadian sojourn, I took a class called 'The Christian Imagination'. Regent College is the kind of place you can learn theology through poetry and painting, alongside the usual hard-to-pronounce disciplines on offer at your more run-of-the-mill seminaries: hermeneutics, exegetics, eschatology and scatology (OK, maybe not that one). I'd become friends with an artist, Linda, who had floaty grey hair and the softest voice you ever heard. She paid a peppercorn rent on a magical house on the edge of the water in exchange for nominal park management duties. There was definitely a west coast vibe about her – she had trees planted on placentas dotted around her garden and kept her paperwork and bills stored under a mohair blanket in the middle of her living room. One time she was about to be evicted because she'd not been able to afford the rent on top of other expenses. She'd reached the conclusion that there was nothing to be done and was on the floor doing just that, nothing, when there was a knock at the door. 'I'm from *Beyond Belief*,' said the woman on the doorstep, once Linda had levered herself off the floor to see who was there. The TV producer wanted to pay a lot of money to use the house as the location of a new four-part drama. It was a pretty amazing miracle, although unfortunately said drama was about a single lady living in a remote park, who got brutally murdered. Linda made the mistake of watching it and then couldn't sleep a night alone for months. She was OK on the rent front though.

When I first met Linda she was making art out of dryer lint. People would gather fluff from the filters of their dryers and she'd make pieces that perhaps had more meaning to them than obvious aesthetic appeal. I sort of understood, or at least I wanted to. It had to do with community, and I was all about community. It was my word *du jour*. Plus, I also wanted to be arty. So when it came to doing my final project for the class, I decided to do a painting, and I went to stay at Linda's in hopes that creating my piece in her bona-fide artist's studio, a glass box suspended in a slightly unnerving fashion over the Pacific, would give me the gumption to actually do the thing. I might have wanted to be arty, but I knew I wasn't a true artist like Linda.

What I made that day was a fairly big picture, using some technique Linda taught me which, as I recall, involved blowing soapy water all over your work just after you'd got it looking exactly as you wanted it. It was a bit of a stretch for my controlling self, but I was 'committed to the process', as Linda would have put it. My picture was of a tree with exposed roots, and the tree was suspended in outer space, with psychedelic flares shooting out of it to show how exciting and positive it was for the tree to be in this unusual setting. It was a metaphor for my place in the world, and I honestly saw nothing wrong with it (with the metaphor I mean, not the picture; the picture was an ugly mess). When I presented it to the class, my professor was kind but concerned. A tree cannot live in space, he said. Its roots need to be in soil.

I had had an unsettled few years, and I felt untethered. Somewhere along the way I'd decided to spin this in a positive light – I wasn't homeless; I was free to travel. I wasn't disconnected and alone; I was able to connect, albeit loosely, to any number of places and people. I wasn't confined to a specific home: the whole world was my home. The positive picture I was trying to paint concealed a rather desolate conclusion that I didn't belong anywhere – and never would. My professor's words were challenging and comforting in equal measure, and from that moment I sought to bed my roots down as deeply and securely as I knew how in Vancouver. And when I left Vancouver, the roots would go down in new soil. As they bedded in, though, I rediscovered the old feelings of homesickness. I'd taken the risk of bonding somewhere, and so of course it hurt to leave. But on balance, I'm with Tennyson: it is indeed 'better to have loved and lost than never to have loved at all'.

Man on the move

Old Testament Israelites were deeply rooted in the stories of their ancestors. It was through these stories that they understood their identity, purpose and place. King David was born around five hundred years after the death of

Moses, but the stories of Moses' life would have shaped him as profoundly as if they'd been contemporaries. I like to think David's homesickness was mitigated somewhat by his forefather's experiences.

Moses – he of the Ten Commandments – was born into a family and a nation living as slaves to their hosts. His people had been promised a land four hundred years earlier, but famine had driven them to Egypt, and there they had stayed – until staying was their only option. Egypt was never home for the Israelites, but memories of the promise must have grown dimmer with each new generation born in captivity.

Moses' life was under threat from the moment his mother lifted him slippery and purple to the light and saw he was a boy. Newborn Israelite boys were to be thrown into the Nile in a brutish effort at population control. Into the Nile he went at three months old, but in a waterproofed papyrus basket, floating among the reeds. A tiny baby doesn't know he has been abandoned in order to save his life. He just knows he is crying and no one comes. But then Pharaoh's daughter saw the basket, heard the cries and felt sorry for this vulnerable Hebrew scrap, alive against the odds. He became hers, albeit given back to his mother for the hard work of broken nights, toilet training and toddler tantrums. He was raised in the palace, son and heir to the oppressors of his people, until he snapped under the strain and before he knew it was on the run for murder. He fled Egypt to Midian, where he stayed for forty years, naming his son Gershom, 'saying, "I have become a foreigner in a foreign land"' (Exodus 2:22).

Nor was this a settled life; pasture for the flocks he tended was hard to come by and he traversed great expanses of wilderness. It was in this wilderness that he came across the flaming bush that did not burn, and was sent by the voice of God, 'I Am', back to Egypt to negotiate Israelite emancipation, ultimately bringing them back into this same wilderness for the final forty years of his life. Moses was a man without a land, belonging to a people without a land. Abandoned to save his life, his own people later rejected him for committing murder in their defence. He was adopted by a new people, only for God to tell him to leave them. Having rescued the Israelites, he spent his last four decades under canvas, constantly on the move. What would Moses have said to the chap by the buffet table, making small talk over his hummus and carrot sticks? I can imagine him giving a wry smile, brushing a stray crisp from his splendid beard and saying, 'Where's home, you ask? I've always thought of home as wherever I'm with God.' And then he'd catch me, red-eyed, listening intently to the exchange, and he'd give me the kind of look that said, 'I understand. It hurts. But you are not alone.'

If anyone should have been prone to homesickness, it was Moses. This must have been a comfort to David, who had good reason for his own struggles. David was born and raised in Bethlehem. His father Jesse is referred to as an 'Ephrathite', a member of a clan within the tribe of Judah that hailed from Bethlehem (the old name for Bethlehem was Ephratha). He had as much claim to belong in Bethlehem as Gary does to Chesterfield, and we know that's saying something. I'm sure, growing up the youngest of eight boys with the job of looking after the family flocks, he had no expectation of ever leaving the area.

And then, one day, he was called in from the pastures for a mysterious encounter with the nation's most senior priest. Samuel took one look at him and announced he was God's choice to replace Israel's first king, Saul, who had begun to go off the rails. There was no clue as to how or when this replacement would take place, so David went back to his sheep. He was too young even to take part in a battle against the Philistines in which his brothers fought some time later, but he was allowed to take them provisions. It was while on one of these bread-and-cheese runs that events took a turn that would remove David from everything he'd known. How could the boy who'd slain the giant champion of his people's enemies with a sling and some pebbles just go quietly back home?

With no idea about David's calling to succeed him, Saul summoned David to the palace as a musician. Saul was in dire need of music therapy, but David's playing, skilled as he was on the harp, only made him feel worse. David was in Saul's service for seven years, until his early twenties, and his success as a warrior – and consequent popularity with the ladies in particular, Saul's daughter Michal among them – drove Saul quite literally crazy with jealousy. David was used to defending himself from wild animals in the wilderness, but in the palace he had to be alert for spears thrown at his head and poison in his wine, at the same time as being repeatedly deployed to the frontline of conflict after conflict. No one feels at home somewhere they are in fear for their life. Regardless of the excitement and his triumphs, these were difficult years for David.

Saul grew more and more obsessed with seeing David killed, and eventually David had to go on the run. No one offered him sanctuary, and he spent the next fifteen years or so as a fugitive, hiding in caves, constantly on the move in the wilderness, and then throwing in his lot with an enemy of Israel. It must have hurt to leave the land he believed God had destined him to lead. He must have wondered when he'd be able to come home; when this king, who only showed his unsuitability more clearly every time he made another attempt at eliminating David, would ever lose the throne. If you've read any of David's songs, you'll know David hit the depths during that time. He felt frightened, alone, angry and lost. He was spitting mad with God for not stepping in and defending him, for making him wait with no sign of progress as year after year went by. He was homesick and desperately tired of always travelling but never arriving.

In some ways, David's adult life is like a play in two acts. When Saul finally died, the change was complete: he became the king he'd been preparing to be since Samuel's anointing. He chose a capital city, built a palace, and his family grew. He had ups and downs, but there were long years of settled success. David ended his life as king of a prosperous and stable country, dying in his bed in his own palace, at peace with the God who had been his security and comfort throughout good times and bad.

Homesickness is painful, and our instinct is to run from

feeling pain, to try and find a way to make it stop. I once had the honour of meeting a man called Dr Paul Brand. He spent his career working with leprosy patients and, with the help of Philip Yancey, he wrote the hugely influential book *Pain: The Gift That Nobody Wants*. Dr Brand has seen first-hand the horrors that result when there is no ability to feel pain. Pain, he says, alerts us to vital information. We mustn't numb pain; we must listen to it.

So what can we learn from the pain of homesickness? What might it be telling us? I think it tells us that we have a need that isn't being met; that we haven't sufficiently embraced the people we are with and the places we find ourselves, in the here and now; that we have allowed ourselves to dwell in the past or to hold out for a distant future. When we are homesick, we need to rethink our understanding of home. And a good place to start is with our family of origin.

CHAPTER TWO

On board the kinship
My family is my home

Family outing to Red Rocks, Merseyside

Why any kid would want to be an orphan is beyond me.

Miss Hannigan, *Annie the Musical*

OUR EARLY LIVES have a kind of mythical haziness to them. We rely on third-person accounts of what happened and how we might have felt about it. We form pictures from family fables and washed-out photographs, images that have the semblance of memory but with fairy-tale distortions – ginormous chairs, uncles who threw ladles of custard at the walls to amuse us, great slobbery dogs the size of donkeys knocking us over when we could barely

29

walk. For good or ill, we can't remember much of what happens to us before we are four or five, but the stories matter. What actually happened matters too.

Research shows that even if we have no conscious memory of experiences in our early years, those experiences have profound repercussions in later life. John Bowlby's work with traumatised children in the 1930s led him to explore the significance of early bonds with caregivers. In the aftermath of World War II, he was asked to present a paper to the World Health Organization on how to best help children left as orphans or homeless. His pamphlet, 'Maternal Care and Mental Health' (1951), became the basis for his Attachment Theory, a psychological model still widely used to understand relational dynamics.[1] Bowlby's research led him to argue that for a child to grow up feeling secure, confident and able to form healthy relationships, they need to form a primary attachment in early babyhood.

For small children, home means family. In the simplest sense, family means the people we belong to by ties of blood, love and loyalty; those who are around day in, day out, meeting our needs. We have an expectation of society being built on units of two parents and their biological offspring, but this setup is less and less common. The American social critic and moralist Christopher Lasch was one of the many voices bewailing the erosion of family structures from the Industrial Revolution onwards. He argued that the family was the primary agency of a child's socialisation, instilling ethical and social norms and profoundly shaping their character.

'The family instills modes of thought and action that become habitual,' he wrote. 'Because of its enormous influence, it colors all of a child's subsequent experience.'[2] But he believed the traditional family unit of married parents and children was under threat from as early as the mid-1800s. He argued it was assailed by capitalism – which took production out of the home, specialising and collectivising skills – and the subsequent intrusion of 'experts' into private life: doctors, teachers, psychiatrists, social workers and lawyers. Between 1870 and 1920, he pointed out, divorce rates in the US increased fifteen-fold, the birth rate fell steadily, women's role in society grew to encompass far more than motherhood, and a moral revolution began which threw assumptions about sexual behaviour to the wind.

The feminist in me can't let Lasch blame family breakdown on women escaping the kitchen without a comeback. We mustn't forget that the idea of motherhood as a full-time – really the only worthwhile – vocation for a woman only existed for a small window of time in a small part of the world, reaching its pinnacle in 1950s America. She-who-is-to-be-praised in Proverbs 31 is a mother, but also a farmer, a tradeswoman, a property tycoon and a philanthropist. My friend Amy has worked part-time while raising her children. When women who don't have jobs outside the home refer to themselves as 'full-time mothers', it makes her furious. 'What does that make me?' she fumed, when this phrase came up recently. 'A part-time mother? I am a mother all the time, too.'

Families come in all shapes and sizes, and social patterns

will always remain in flux. What really matters for the child's sense of home, it seems to me, is a safe, close bond with one or two adults who can be relied on to be around in a consistent way, meeting physical and emotional needs as they arise.

Jackpot

If life is a lottery, I drew a lucky ticket.

I was born in what my girls refer to as 'the olden days'. My birth was not announced on social media, there is no film footage of me as a child, my mother did not blog about my bowel movements and developing aptitudes in the areas of speech and food consumption, and it would not be too hard to eliminate all evidence of the bowl haircut that graced my head until I was six. However, my parents are fine story-tellers, my dad took photos and developed them himself in the bathroom, and my mother kept a diary and regularly updated a family treasure known as 'The Remarks Book' with her children's early witticisms. So I do have a good idea of how things were before I started remembering them for myself.

My life has been blessed by the knowledge that I was hoped and planned for. My mother's great ambition in life was to have children and, as Disney might have put it, I was her dream come true. I've been told over and over again of how they prayed for me as I grew in the womb and loved me before they met me (and after, I'm happy to report).

I met up with my mum for a coffee recently and talk turned to my birth. It was long and traumatic for both of us, eighteen hours culminating in a breech delivery and several weeks in special care. She worries it might have scarred me. She recounted again – one of those stories I never tire of hearing – how she came round from the anaesthetic, felt her stomach and, realising she'd given birth, frantically asked where her baby was. 'They brought you to me and that was it – we were together from that moment.' In this retelling she's choosing to miss out the bit where she left me alone in hospital on my first Christmas to go out for lunch with friends. Maybe I am a bit scarred after all.

I was scrawny and wrinkly, and by all accounts a squawker, but my love-blinded parents couldn't have been more pleased with me. When I was discharged from hospital they took me home in our green Morris Minor, through melting snow, to our house in the grounds of Christ's Hospital, a slightly unusual public school in the depths of West Sussex. My dad was a house tutor and English teacher, while my mum had happily given up teaching to devote herself to motherhood (i.e. me).

Last week I was heading home after a weekend with friends in Sussex, and drove past a road sign saying 'Christ's Hospital – 2 miles'. I nearly drove onto the verge in my excitement. Part of me had always wondered if this school was as fictional as Hogwarts. My mental picture of the place was somewhat strange: pupils dressed in archaic floor-length gowns, processing through formal gardens playing brass instruments – and me, being pushed along in a vast Silver Cross pram, squawking. The road sign was the glass shoe that proved the little girl's adventures in fairyland were not a dream, but actually happened.

Teaching was not a good fit for my dad. He'd fallen into it after graduation from Cambridge, for want of a better idea of what to do, and quickly discovered that he had none of the sense of vocation needed to make a go of it. After a period of soul-searching he was approved for ordination in the Church of England, and began the requisite two years of study plus three years in a training post, or 'curacy' as it's called. This is still pretty much what happens now if you want to be a vicar, as I was explaining to my friend Becky the other day. She's not met many church people in her life, and she's full of questions. 'That's a lot of training,' she mused. 'Kind of like a doctor. I've never thought about it before, but I suppose vicars have quite an important role, so it's good they are properly prepared before being let loose on a church.'

During our two years in Bristol, while my dad did his training, we lived in a flat at the top of a big house in Clifton, near Bristol Zoo. Family lore has it that at night you could sometimes hear lions roar. My sister's arrival shortly after I turned two was not the trauma it is for some firstborns. I showed no signs of feeling neglected and was happy to share the limelight. Another of my mum's oft-repeated stories is how – when she was pregnant with Esther – she worried about how she could possibly find love for another child when she was full to capacity with love for me, and then found her love doubled and there was enough for both of us. I hoard these stories like gemstones.

I had a big party for my second birthday; twelve friends, in smocked dresses or brown corduroy dungarees, and a pink cake shaped like a butterfly. The photo shows most of the children sitting rather solemnly around a table heaving with party food, while my cousin Hannah and I sat underneath it eating Smarties.

Actual memory begins to mingle with the stories and photographs at some stage during our three years in Upton, Merseyside, where my dad did his curacy. When I think about that time, blurry and slightly surreal images pass through my mind. There's me falling downstairs with my toy trolley, colourful wooden bricks flying in all directions. Me with a wodge of green Plasticine on my head, which had to be chopped out along with chunks of my hair. I vividly remember making the decision to put it there, although the reasoning escapes me now. And there I am, posting little objects into the hole in my dad's guitar, and asking Mark from the youth group to marry me, and walking up the brutal incline of our street with achy legs. On a recent visit back to explore the old neighbourhood, I discovered rather disconcertingly that the house was at the bottom of the most gentle of slopes. I can only conclude there must have been a major geological event at some point during the past thirty years.

The memories begin to come thick and fast after that. I'm standing outside the Lavins's house and Joy is peeping out of the circular window in her front door, mouthing, 'Not Jo again!' which gave me a warm feeling in my tummy because I understood it meant she was beyond delighted to see me. I'm making sure my head is on the white rabbit not the black one on my pillowcase, because the white rabbit gives me good dreams. I'm in Joey Elliot's back garden drinking slightly too strong orange squash on a hot afternoon; I'm shouting to make echoes in the concrete tunnel that leads to the playground. When my mum was expecting my brother, I remember thinking he was sitting on a small blue chair in her stomach waiting patiently to be born. I also remember finding it hard to get my parents' full attention, and desperately trying to come up with interesting topics of conversation. They were hugely stretched, with three children under five and a busy church to run.

It was busy and noisy but we had meals at the kitchen table together every day. Most days began in a riotous jumble in my parents' bed and ended with a story, a pray and a cuddle. We had outings to Red Rocks beach with a primus stove and sausages to cook on it – they featured in most of our forays to the great outdoors; and we laughed a lot. I had a secure home within my family.

The unsafe family

I've painted a rosy picture here, but I know that legions of babies are born into hostile, unsafe situations, where no one is waiting for them with happy expectation and there are no drawers of carefully folded onesies. My friend Helen fosters babies taken away from their mothers at birth; once she was given three babies, born nine months apart from each other to the same woman, a woman with raging addictions and a chaotic lifestyle that left her unable to care for her children. A family in our church adopted twins of seven years old who'd lived with numerous foster carers in their short lives, removed from their mother at age two to protect them from her abusive boyfriend. They were fortunate to find a permanent home, more fortunate than most of their nine siblings.

Worse are the stories of newborns left on doorsteps, found on rubbish heaps, in ditches, in public toilets. I heard a man on the radio this week talking about finding a baby in a phone box. What of these babies? Some never get over it – there are too many tragic stories of those whose lives are irreparably damaged. But there are also stories of unbelievable wholeness and redemption – people who don't have at all the story you might expect given the way their first chapter went.

Half a world and a whole universe away from where I was starting out on life with all the advantages of knowing I was loved and wanted, my now-husband Shawn was nineteen months old and already a seasoned survivor.

Shawn's mother, Rita, was raised in Idaho with her two older brothers, her salesman father and housewife mother. She was beautiful, spirited and volatile and, by her early teens, her behaviour was getting her into serious trouble. Diagnosed years later with bipolar disorder, there are clear signs her mental health struggles began early; she attempted suicide at sixteen. There followed two years shut away in an institution. On her release, she hit the hippy trail, finding escape in alcohol, drugs and free love. After a near-fatal motorbike accident when she was twenty-one, doctors told her she would never bear children. Shawn was conceived a year later during a brief fling. He met his father when he was twelve and they've had intermittent contact since, but nothing substantial.

Rita's parents were horrified to discover she was pregnant and begged her to abort the baby. Shawn has seen journal entries and poems Rita wrote at the time as she wrestled over whether to keep him in the face of strong opposition. The story told to Shawn, therefore, is not only that he wasn't planned, but that his future grandparents were so afraid for him they'd rather he'd never been born.

Shawn was born two months prematurely in Minneapolis. His middle name, Douglas, was given him by a friend of Rita's who visited them in hospital. He was one of her group of friends who'd shared needles and given each other hepatitis, and he's since died. Babies have a 50 per cent chance of contracting hepatitis from their mothers; dodging yet another bullet, Shawn was one of the half who don't. Rita went home after a couple of weeks, but Shawn had to stay until he grew bigger and stronger. She visited when she could, but the hospital was several bus rides away.

Shawn doesn't have many photographs of himself as a baby. The couple he has show a solemn little chap in a grubby baby-grow – big blue eyes, wide, serious and direct. It breaks my heart to think about what he'd already had to overcome, what those eyes had already seen.

Rita became involved with a violent alcoholic, Rick, and they entered into an ill-judged marriage when Shawn was two. Rita once told me the story of how she tried to escape out of the bathroom window on the morning of her wedding. Her father pulled her back inside and marched her weeping down the aisle, presumably convinced this marriage was in his daughter's best interest. Rick disappeared on a three-day bender as soon as the vows were exchanged. The marriage lasted four years, and they had a son and a daughter together.

Shawn's earliest memories are of being left alone in frightening places, of seeing his mother beaten and feeling powerless to defend her, and of perpetual hunger. The family survived on food stamps and welfare handouts, but where drug and alcohol dependency is concerned, milk, cheese and fresh fruit are never the priority. Rita loved her children, but her addictions played havoc with her good intentions and she wasn't able to provide them with adequate care. When I first became a mother, I had to deal with some strong emotions about Shawn's early life. The fierce instinct to do whatever it took to protect and nurture our tiny newborn daughter was overwhelming, and I had moments of profound anger that the person who should have shielded Shawn put him at risk over and over again. It took me time to forgive the wrong that had been done to the man I loved. The irony of Shawn comforting me as I wept about what he'd gone through as a child did not escape us!

While much of Shawn's childhood was chaotic at best, there were interludes of sanity spent with his grandparents and with Scott and Debbie, his aunt and uncle and their two children. The wider family had some awareness of the context he'd return to after these visits, but Rita was careful to conceal the full picture. When Shawn and I have talked with Scott and Debbie about what Shawn's childhood was like, they've expressed shock and regret that they did not do more for him at the time, but they'll probably never fully know the positive impact they had on his life. I sat next to a lawyer at a wedding last December who represents vulnerable children in court cases. He told me dysfunction escalates generation to generation, unless a child has a reasonable degree of exposure to a healthy model of family. I'm sure the times Shawn stayed with his grandparents and uncle and aunt are the reason he is such an improbably wonderful husband and father, and I will always be grateful to them.

The family lived for a while in a remote farmhouse, scene of some of the worst horrors of Shawn's childhood. He was able to roam where he pleased, and there was a tree he'd climb, spending hours in its leafy sanctuary. He says now that this was where he first experienced the presence of God, there in the tree; wrapping the small, traumatised boy around with peace and comfort. On a trip back to Minneapolis with our girls, we went looking for the tree. The farmhouse is long gone and the suburbs have sprawled over the wilderness, but we still looked for it. Alexa, our older daughter, was four at the time, the age her dad had been when he'd moved to the farmhouse. We wouldn't have allowed Alexa out of our sight, let alone let her disappear for whole days at a time.

Eventually Rita found the extraordinary courage she needed to take her three children and flee. They lived for a while in a women's refuge, before being allocated government housing. But it wasn't long before Rita became involved with another abusive man, and then another, and the drama continued. Over Shawn's childhood there were restraining orders on three different men. They moved constantly, from one bleak estate to another in the suburbs of south Minneapolis, sometimes living with several other families, other times in apartments barely fit for habitation.

Shawn had to learn fast about how to look after himself. He began earning his own money when he was ten, using it for food, clothing and toothpaste. He joined the Crips, a US-wide street gang, when he was sixteen. He told me this on our first date, as we walked along the beach below West Point Grey in Vancouver in the dead of night. I was suddenly hyperaware of the fact there were no other people in earshot and I had only known this man for three weeks. He assured me, however, that he was no longer the dangerous gangster of his youth, and I decided to believe him – the alternative being to make a run for it, crying for my mummy and/or a Mountie.[3] Shawn became a Christian when he was seventeen, through the ex-girlfriend of a fellow gang member, whom he'd followed to church in an effort to impress her enough to become her next boyfriend. On his second visit, he heard for the first time that he could have a clean, forgiven start because Jesus had died for him. He went home, prayed a prayer from a booklet he'd been given at the end of the service and flushed his entire supply of pot down the toilet. That night his life set off on a new trajectory – one that would one day put him, against all the odds, in my path.

Shawn is an extraordinary person. He is strong, bright, focused and very funny. A reference for a job he went for in his mid-twenties said he was 'a trophy of God's grace'. Only God's intervention and Shawn's God-given character could possibly account for the man he has become – a loving and committed husband and father, a church leader and degree-level theology lecturer, an emotionally healthy and sunny-natured human being. Rita also met God along the way. These days she's doing well, living a quiet life in North Dakota near Shawn's sister and her grandchildren.

I'm so grateful Shawn allowed me to tell his story here, because he is testament to the fact that no one is a slave to any principle of cause and effect. Finding home is more challenging for those with a rocky start, but it is entirely possible.

Jesse and Sons

We don't have any record of David's early life, but we are told some things about his family. He was the youngest of eight boys, which might make one wonder if his mother was trying for a girl, except there are two sisters mentioned in 2 Chronicles 2:16. There is no mention of David's mother and, given that it would be three thousand years or so before Bowlby came along and told us all how important it is for a baby to bond with a primary caregiver, we can't assume he got the cuddles he needed. After all those babies, perhaps she gave newborn David a peck on the forehead and handed him over to a wet nurse with a sense of hearty relief.

As the youngest son, David was so low down the pecking order that when Samuel the prophet-priest came to Bethlehem to anoint one of Jesse's boys as God's future king of Israel, it didn't even occur to Jesse to bring him in from the fields. Even after his anointing, David's brothers continued to treat him as an annoying little brat. There was no chance they were going to let him get big-headed about it. When he showed up to bring food to his three oldest siblings, Eliab, Abinadab and Shammah, who were with the Israelite army facing off against the Philistines, David hung about asking awkward questions. How could the Israelite soldiers allow God's name to be dishonoured, he wanted to know? What would the man who defeated Goliath get by way of reward? Overhearing him, Eliab did what older brothers the world over would have done – gave him a roasting and tried to squash him back into place. 'Get lost, shrimp. You're just trying to get a front row view of the fighting.'⁴ To which David replied, 'Now what have I done? Can't I even speak?'⁵ – springing out of the way just in time to avoid a dead arm no doubt.

It's probably fair to say that David's family of origin was perfectly fine, particularly for those psychologically unenlightened times. He may not have been cossetted and cooed over, snuggled and adored (although who's to say he wasn't?), but he was certainly secure in the knowledge that he was the youngest son of Jesse. The thing about David, though, was that, as he grew from child to man, his relationship with God came to be of far greater significance than that with his family. The Spirit of the Lord came on him when Samuel anointed him, and remained with him from that day on.[6] God became his security, his refuge, his shield, his rock, his stronghold – his family and his home. This is not to say family was not significant to David, or that it shouldn't be to us. Lived experience tells us that it is, let alone all those studies that have been done to back up the theory. But his family didn't define his life. His definition of family changed as he became more spiritually alive.

Family redefined

Twenty-eight generations later, Jesus, son of Joseph (but really Son of God), was born, a branch on the same family tree. In Luke's gospel, there's an account of Jesus at around thirty years old, apparently disowning his mother and brothers, who'd come to see him but couldn't get anywhere close because of the crowds. Word got passed to him: 'Hey, your family's here.' And he said, 'My mother and brothers are those who hear God's word and put it into practice.'[7] This is not the harsh brush-off it might seem at first reading, but a redrawing of the parameters of family. Jesus was instituting a new family, the family of God, to which anyone can belong. As Paul wrote to the Romans, 'For those who are led by the Spirit of God are the children of God . . . The Spirit himself testifies with our spirit that we are God's children.'[8] For those, like Shawn, who've experienced rejection and damage at the hands of their human parents, there is comfort in the knowledge that in some mysterious yet certainly not abstract or intangible sense, God is their parent too.

The writer Donald Miller grew up without a father, an experience he explores in his book *To Own a Dragon*.[9] He had some initial frustrations with God-as-father, having witnessed the ways human fathers had enriched the lives of his friends with sports coaching, advice on girls and funds to help pay for college. As he puts it, he wanted God to 'step out of heaven and show me how to work a power saw'.[10] What he gradually came to understand was that although God might not cheer him on from the side lines of his baseball games, he did help Donald to know who he was and what he was designed to become. He did want Donald to be intimately involved with him, and to call him by the most familiar of terms – 'Abba', or Dad. He did want him to submit to his authority and discipline, to know his practical provision – daily bread and suchlike – and most of all, he wanted Donald to know how totally, completely and overwhelmingly he was loved. This was a wonderful discovery, and went some way to healing his wounded, fatherless self. But he's honest about the reality – that this life, even with God in it, is never neat and tidy: 'The feeling a person who grows up without a father has is that God is disinterested. It's a difficult feeling to explain, because I also believe God is loving and good and involved. But there is a doubt, you know, a feeling He is somehow removed.'[11] So yes, God is our father. But, for better or worse, our human families shape us too.

So what is a family? Of course in one sense family is made up of our blood relations – mother, father, siblings, grandparents and so on – all those people who share our distinctive flared left nostril and hairy toes. But Jesus' definition seems to radically restate our innate human understanding of who has responsibility for us and for whom we have responsibility. He didn't just teach that God is our father, but that his followers are brothers and sisters. Christians are connected to other Christians with stronger ties than the bonds of biology. The implications of this are profound. As Rodney Clapp writes with iconoclastic panache, 'The family is not God's most important institution on earth. The family is not the social agent that most significantly shapes and forms the characters of Christians. The family is not the primary vehicle of God's grace and salvation for a waiting, desperate world.'[12] God's plan to bless the world began with Abraham's biological family, but it was always working towards the creation of a family that belongs together because of love, not genetics. Given the complications, the brokenness, the pain so many of us experience in the context of our biological families, shifting the focus of our understanding of family is potentially a positive adjustment.

Childish dreams

When people have asked my mum and dad about the impact all our moving about had on their children, they've often said that we were at home where they were. I'm sure this is largely true. I hope for the sake of my own girls that a child's home is wherever their parents are. They are six and nine, and living in their third house. They often refer casually to their next house, expressing hopes that it might be near a sweet shop – or have its own swimming pool. Not with a vicar for a dad, I tell them. God's our father too, Alexa once countered, and he'll give you anything if you ask – even a caravan. I've no idea why a caravan was the best thing she could think to ask for at that moment, but I admired her faith.

What is for sure is that I was hugely fortunate to have parents who were 100 per cent committed to each other and to me and my siblings. By and large I took the moving in my stride. But as we geared up to our move to Portugal, when I was five, I had a recurring nightmare that tells me I was affected by the change at some level. In the nightmare, I would be standing on the road outside our church, and I'd look down and see a crack. The crack would widen to a chasm, and another one would appear, and then another, until all the ground around me had

47

broken up, leaving me nowhere to stand. And then I'd fall into the darkness.

Home is family, but home is not just family. It is time to add another piece to the puzzle.

CHAPTER THREE

Welcome to my world

My culture is my home

Cruzinha

My culture is my identity and personality. It gives me spiritual, intellectual and emotional distinction from others, and I am proud of it.

M. F. Moonzajer

WE DID NOT move to the Algarve for the sun or the white sandy beaches. We moved there for the birds. My dad had been fascinated by ornithology since childhood, and had become increasingly disturbed by signs that all was not well in the natural world. Throughout his curacy, his sense that good stewardship of the earth was a fundamental aspect of being a Christian grew stronger, as did his dismay at the general ambivalence in the church towards what was clearly becoming a catastrophic neglect of the planet. He felt compelled to respond, and 'A Rocha', a Christian environmental conservation charity, came into being in 1983.

Portugal had been the destination of choice for this fledgling organisation for several reasons. First, just under forty years of the oppressive regime of António de Oliveira Salazar had ended in the early 1970s, and a thriving tourism industry was springing up in the newly liberated economy. Hotels, villas and apartment blocks were gobbling up pristine coastline with voracious speed. The Algarve is a key stopover for migratory birds, but their habitats were fast disappearing. Developers and the government officials issuing permits could not have cared less about the environmental impact of this lucrative building spree.

Second, the Protestant church was small, fragile and under-resourced. The A Rocha team would do what they could to encourage the local Christian community. And third, while it was a decade or more before the concept of cheap air travel really took hold, Portugal was relatively accessible from England, and it would be possible for us to maintain ties with friends, family and the charity's network of supporters.

Of course, at the age of five I knew none of this. All I knew was that we were off on an adventure. One day in early September we landed at Faro Airport as the sun set, leaving behind it a fuchsia sky the like of which I had never seen before. The air was hot and heavy with dust, loaded with the smell of thyme, fennel and rosemary. We were picked up by Tom, a Scottish teacher we'd met on our recce trip that February, who piled the five of us and our luggage into his battered Renault Four and drove us to his home, where we spent the first night in our new country.

Our first house in Portugal was in the town of Armação de Pêra. Mum remembers it as dark and gloomy, full of over-sized and grotesquely ornate furniture, and so damp in winter that clothes became mouldy in the cupboards. It was next to a discotheque which throbbed and pulsed into the small hours, and when it rained, the street outside became a treacherous and fast-flowing brown stream. But I was genuinely shocked by this adult perspective the first time my mother shared it. I loved the fact that we had a flat roof to play on, complete with a grey concrete washing tub that for some reason captivated my imagination as much as any Wendy house or science kit. I slept in a double bed with a fancy iron bedstead, in a room that had a skylight in place of a window. I'd discovered that Portuguese people loved children, especially blond ones, and if you stared at the jar of chocolate umbrellas with enough longing, the shopkeeper would give you one. The painful twist of the cheeks that came with the gift was a small price to pay.

Even at that early age I recognised there were advantages to being a cultural oddity. No one expected you to adhere to societal convention; you were excused for the times you offended the more subtle social niceties, and when you got something important wrong it would be explained in a kindly manner. One of the hardest things for me about being in England even now is that I am supposed to know how to behave. I look and sound English, and I have come a long way in terms of learning what Englishness means, but I commit cultural faux-pas on a regular basis. In a strange way, when I am somewhere I don't belong, that's when there's a sense of comfort, of familiarity.

We had our first Portuguese Christmas in the Armação house. There were advent calendars with glittery nativity scenes, a tree, and Father Christmas delivered the stockings to our new location without mishap. In all the years we lived in Portugal, Christmas remained a traditionally English affair for our family. No salt cod or present-giving on Christmas Eve for us. Of course, what we realised once we began sharing our Christmases with our adopted family from the A Rocha community was that Christmas traditions are very different from family to family, let alone between cultures, even if they do revolve around the same elements. How, when and what gifts were given was a matter for heated debate year after year, with everyone claiming their way was the right way. We so often assume our culture to be normative. Although the discovery that this is not the case wasn't a comfortable process, I'm grateful I went through it: it has given me an open-minded appreciation for the vast cultural diversity of our shared world.

I started at the International School of the Algarve as soon as we got to Portugal, catching the school bus on the beachfront each morning. Because of the way the school systems correlated (or rather, didn't), I was in a class with children two years my senior. My seven-year-old classmates were a wild lot. I listened with naïve incomprehension to stories of what they got up to at weekends: discos and kissing competitions, minimal parental supervision, all-age alcohol-fuelled craziness. I didn't fit in, and while they spent lunchtimes discussing horror films, gambling with marbles or trying to make each other faint, I made dens by myself in the fig orchard. For a while I had a friend called Samantha, who ate half of my packed lunch every day in addition to her own. Once I had a mini Mars Bar, an exotic rarity sent all the way from England; she ate half of that too.

There were fourteen nationalities represented in my class. I quickly realised that of all the places you could come from, England was the least cool. Those of us of English extraction downplayed the fact and joined in the general mockery of our motherland with more gusto than necessary in order to be clear we disdained it as much as the next person. But when I went back to England for the first time, it felt gloriously like home. And when people asked me whether I preferred England or Portugal, which they did, over and over again, I said England without hesitation.

During our first summer in Portugal, Mum and Dad did a language course at the university in Coimbra. We stayed in part of a large, stone house with high ceilings and long echoing halls. I have three particularly vivid memories from that interlude. One was the time we arrived back at the house in the late afternoon. My younger siblings

Esther and Jeremy had fallen asleep in the car and they got carried in. Feeling this was unfair, as I was tired too, I pretended to sleepwalk into the house. My understanding of how a person sleepwalked was to close my eyes and hold my arms out in front of me. I walked straight into a giant cactus, palms first, and the next few hours were spent extracting a million tiny splinters from my hands. Then there was the evening the ex-husband of the lady who lived in the other part of the house came back to beat her. Dad barricaded himself with us in our bedroom, and we had to listen to the horrific sound of her screams. The last thing was my brother falling into a well as we packed up to leave. Perhaps because it was such an eventful time, I was shocked to find out just recently that we weren't there long at all – a matter of weeks. In my memory, this was one of my childhood homes. I was talking about this time-distortion with my friend Lisa recently, and she told me that when she was four, her mother had left, supposedly on a short holiday to Florida, when actually she had run away with her father's best friend. Until last year my friend had thought that she hadn't seen her mother for two years. It was five weeks.

After a few months in Armação, we moved up the coast to a village called Mexilhoeira Grande[1] because the nearby headland had become a likely location for the dreamed-of study centre. Our village home was a light and airy flat above a hairdresser's. To get to the outside stairs that took you up to our front door, you had to navigate past Oscar the guard dog. His headlong charge to the extremity of his chain, fangs bared and hoarse bark echoing down the passageway, was a daily ordeal.

We children soon befriended our neighbour, who said good morning to us so cheerily that we christened her 'The Bom Dia Lady'. We'd spend hours lingering in our front yard hoping she would give us dried figs, which she very often did. We'd also get invited into the hair salon on occasion, to be cooed over by whiskery, black-clad old ladies under hairdryers and given doorstep wedges of bread liberally sprinkled with sugar. If your husband died, you had to wear black for several years to show a respectful degree of sadness. It was one of many things that struck us as quite astonishing at first, but then became the new normal. Like the fact that it wasn't possible to be too late to something, whereas if you arrived on time you'd be the only one there and it would be awkward; and that small lizards would occasionally scuttle across your bedroom wall.

Our next move was precipitated by the unexpected arrival of a new baby in the family. Happy as we all were at her arrival, there was no room for her in the Mexilhoeira flat. By the time Beth was born, we were settled into a bright white Algarvian villa on a semi-built estate in arid scrubland a few miles inland from the town of Carvoeiro. Boa Vista, or 'Beautiful View' as it had been named – by someone who'd clearly never visited – was perhaps lacking a little in aesthetic charm, but it was a wonderful place for a child to roam. There was a hidden dip on the edge of the estate, at the bottom of which lived a wizened old lady in a tumbledown house. There were overgrown vines and almond groves on the boundary of the development, and all kinds of abandoned building supplies, which the local children used to create elaborate playhouses. There was one occasion when the developer arrived to restart work on one of the houses and found his bricks had been repurposed. He angrily demanded that all of us involved in the playhouses project put back everything where he'd left it. Assuming we would be sent to prison, I beetled off to hide under my parents' bed, where I wept hot tears of fear and regret over my poor life choices.

The house in Boa Vista had a flat roof. One night we were woken by Mum and Dad and carried upstairs to where they had laid out sleeping bags, lit candles and made us a midnight feast. Lying on my back in the warm, inky night, I felt as if I had joined one of the constellations. One of the things I feel a real sense of grief about is the lack of sky in my English life – no stargazing, no sitting out to see the sunset through from beginning to end, so rarely the kind of azure blue sky that makes your heart sing and your vision swim with colour overload.

When I was nine, we left Boa Vista and moved to a farmhouse, on the headland by Mexilhoeira, called Cruzinha – a house which was to be our home for nine years. Originally a small, traditional farmhouse, it had been added to over the years; when we moved in, building began on an extension to provide our family with two extra bedrooms in the upstairs flat and an exhibition space for environmental education beneath. In addition to our flat, the house had two dormitories, a double guestroom with a sitting room attached, and a shack half-heartedly converted to a pool house. Much to my dismay, the pool itself was used as a rainwater tank – green, slimy and full of squirmy things.

Over the years our family was joined at Cruzinha by a steady stream of scientists and conservationists, nature lovers, artists and adventurers. There were usually between two and five longer-term members of our community, a constantly varying number of volunteers, and the occasional holidaymaker. When Mum or Dad picked us up from the bus stop after school, our first question would often be, 'Who's at home?', and the answer was always different. The four of us children dealt differently with the comings and goings and the sharing of our space and our parents with so many others. For me it was pure joy. The first time I didn't live in a community setting, in fact, was when I got married. While Shawn was adjusting to living with another person, I was adjusting to living with just one person.

Cruzinha had its own culture. It wasn't Portuguese; it wasn't English. It changed according to who was there but it always retained its own flavour. We had our traditions and our stories; our particular ways of doing things. Washing up was a major social event and often took several hours, amidst hilarity and general tomfoolery. On Sundays those who wanted to would gather and worship. We'd pray and sing, and someone would talk from the Bible. Then we'd have a big barbecue before piling into cars and heading to the beach.

The volunteers, or 'volwols' as they were known, would frequently initiate water fights, card games and chatty tea breaks in between shelling sack-loads of almonds, repainting the wooden blinds or painstakingly transferring data on bird migrations from log books onto the computer. While Rick Astley, Michael Jackson and Neneh Cherry climbed the popular music charts, at Cruzinha we were big fans of a Christian band called Fat and Frantic, friends of one of our assistant wardens, and could be heard belting out the lyrics to 'Last Night My Wife Hoovered My Head' or 'I Was a Teenaged Werewolf' as we nipped along the dirt tracks of the headland in our grubby grey mini-van.

Birds were the major focus of study at Cruzinha in the early years. Dad and others would rise at silly o'clock to open the fine nets they'd put up around the garden – in the pine wood, the citrus orchard, alongside the pond, and in the waist-high grasses of the field in front of the house. The team would do the rounds, extracting their feathered captives and popping them into cloth bags. They'd be weighed, measured and aged before having a small metal band fitted around one leg, and finally they'd be released. My interest in ringing, meanwhile, was purely social. I'd hover around trying to strike up conversations and generally getting in the way. I was more into mammals – specifically the motley crew of dogs we loved and lost over the years. We ended up with a sizeable pet cemetery, where four dogs were memorialised with headstones of scavenged marble, alongside rabbits who had succumbed to myxomatosis, a hamster with a brain tumour, and a handful of baby guinea pigs whose mother wasn't maternally inclined.

Cruzinha was far more than a house; it was a small kingdom – one where I was known and accepted. School continued to be a hostile environment, but this other world was a bigger, brighter place. When I was at home, I wasn't an object of fun that people fought not to have to sit next to; I was part of the action. When I think about which culture feels most like home to me, it would probably still be the Cruzinha culture that existed for those few years.

Third Culture Kids

Moving abroad at the age of five would have huge implications for my growing sense of cultural identity. The term Third Culture Kids (TCKs) was coined in the 1950s by American sociologists John and Ruth Useem to refer to those who spend a significant portion of their developmental years outside their parents' culture.[2] They have a relationship with their parents' culture, and with the culture they live in, but they don't fully belong to either. They are part of a 'third culture', and are likely to identify most with others who've had the same experience: 'Global nomads recognise each other. Regardless of passport held, countries lived in, sponsoring agency differences or age, nomads have a sudden recognition of kinship, a sense of homecoming that underlines the powerful bond of shared culture.'[3]

Third Culture Kids share certain characteristics; some positive, some less so. We are adventurous and accepting

59

of difference. We form immediate connections with people, but are wary about letting anyone near our hearts, as we have said goodbye too many times. We adapt well to new situations, but are sometimes overcome with grief for places we've left. Leaving Portugal, and more particularly Cruzinha, was a form of bereavement for me, and I am still occasionally struck by a horrible sense of loss that can leave me winded and disorientated. In the run-up to transitions I get really anxious, although when it comes to it I take change in my stride; I love seeing the earth from a plane.

TCKs have a broad perspective of the world and an awareness of their own bias; this can sometimes make us arrogant, and it can also make us feel quite lonely. Heidi Sand-Hart is a TCK whose book *Home Keeps Moving* is an account of her experience of growing up in an exotic mix of four cultures, and the impact that has had on her.[4] She writes, 'Limited mind-sets and worldview not only anger but isolate me, leaving me feeling like a misunderstood alien. I feel claustrophobic in a setting where people have spent their whole lives together in the same town. Everyone has a history with each other, and whether there be a slight measure of jealousy, I feel entirely alone. I feel like these sorts of people don't have the capacity to understand me, so they sometimes don't even bother trying.'[5] In this regard I am blessed beyond measure to have three siblings with whom I share memories and cultural reference points. We are closer than the average set of brothers and sisters, and part of that lies in the knowledge that few others in this world can even begin to relate to how and where we grew up.

TCKs struggle with rootlessness and restlessness, vacillating between two competing desires: to settle and to keep moving. As an anonymous writer online expressed it, 'TCKs are marginal, mobile in body, soul, and intellect. Their roots lie in uprootedness. They fit in everywhere, nowhere in particular. They are simultaneously insiders and outsiders.'[6] While Shawn and I have made a conscious and deliberate effort to fight our flightiness, I'm not at all surprised to find myself with one sister living in Kenya, my brother on the remote island of St Helena, and my youngest sister embedded in the Bengali community in East London.

I would not change my upbringing for anything, but I am glad that my girls will have a home within English culture as they grow towards adulthood. They will be able to reminisce with friends about Mr Tumble and Peppa Pig. They will remember the ice-cream van coming down our street – and hopefully laugh about how they thought for years that the tune it played meant it had run out of ice cream (judge if you will, but this little fib saved us hours of whining). The smell of cut grass, bonfires, and honeysuckle will give them the warm feeling of belonging. They are proud of their American passports and dual nationality, but they are English to the core.

The cross-culture Christian

The Merriam-Webster dictionary defines culture as 'the beliefs, customs, arts, etc., of a particular society, group, place, or time; a particular society that has its own beliefs, ways of life, art, etc; a way of thinking, behaving, or working that exists in a place or organization (such as a business)'. We are products of culture, we live in culture – our culture can be our home.

If you've grown up within one culture and never left it for a substantial length of time, it could be that you've never considered the degree to which your culture is your home. If that's the case, now might be an opportune time for reflection. There is something healthy about a close and comfortable identification with one particular culture, but perhaps, especially for those of us who are Christians, a degree of tension is a good thing. Christians by our very nature are 'in the world but not of it'.[7] There are ways in which our values, our behaviour and our choices will – rightly – put us at odds with the *zeitgeist*. By this I don't mean that we should retreat into a ghetto where we only listen to Christian rock music and wear T-shirts printed with shameless plagiarisms of advertising slogans, like 'Jesus – he's the real thing!' What I mean is that we belong to the kingdom of God, in which God's concerns become ours, where we love what he loves and run from what he tells us is dangerous. To a degree we have to work out for ourselves what it is OK to embrace in our culture, and where a commitment to pursue holiness requires us to hold back. There are church communities where leaders lay down the law about everything from jewellery to alcohol, and to how and where it is OK to dance, if ever. And then there are churches where you will never hear a peep from the front about the details of how you live.

Personally I find it helpful to remember that 'the earth is the LORD's and everything in it' (Psalm 24:1); good things like food, sex and recreation can all be distorted and broken if we misuse them, but God made them – and is seriously experienced in the business of redemption.

The biblical narrative begins with a brand-new creation, and tells of the very earliest humans establishing customs, traditions and ways of life. Left to their own devices, aspects of their culture quickly turn dark: 'every inclination of the thoughts of the human heart was only evil all the time' (Genesis 6:5). Many of us will be familiar with the story of the flood, in which all but Noah's family are wiped out. Noah's family became nations which spread out and repopulated the earth, all speaking the same language – until God saw it was making them too strong and arrogant, so he confused things.[8] Abraham, the founder of the nation of Israel, was directly descended from Noah, and Joseph, whose favour with the Egyptian ruler during a time of widespread famine led to the Israelites' prolonged time in Egypt, was Abraham's grandson. Cultures can survive but seldom develop or thrive under slavery. It wasn't until after Israel's dramatic liberation from Pharaoh's oppression that Israel's cultural identity truly formed. The biblical book of Leviticus sits at just this point in the chronology.

Leviticus doesn't have the galloping narrative of Exodus, the poetic allure of Song of Songs or the immediacy of Paul's letters. It's a long list of rules, many of them rather bizarre-sounding to our twenty-first century ears. We rarely come across 'greenish or reddish mould' and, if we

63

did, it certainly wouldn't occur to us to take it to a priest.[9] I have to admit that Shawn regularly trims his beard, in clear violation of Leviticus 19:27, and I eat my steak medium-rare with impunity, Leviticus 19:26 be hanged. Why all these rules? And why don't we pay them much attention anymore?

Leviticus was written for a specific time in Israel's history. These people were newly freed from four hundred years of slavery in Egypt, now wandering the desert learning how to be God's holy, set-apart people before entering the land of Canaan – where they'd be tempted by a whole array of other gods and alternative ways to live. Rather than reading these rules as nit-picking and frivolous, what we should see instead is that life with a holy God impacts absolutely everything. This is how Paul explains it in his letter to the Romans, as rendered in *The Message*:

Take your everyday, ordinary life – your sleeping, eating, going-to-work, and walking-around life – and place it before God as an offering. Embracing what God does for you is the best thing you can do for him. Don't become so well-adjusted to your culture that you fit into it without even thinking. Instead, fix your attention on God. You'll be changed from the inside out. Readily recognise what he wants from you, and quickly respond to it. Unlike the culture around you, always dragging you down to its level of immaturity, God brings the best out of you, develops well-formed maturity in you.[10]

After forty years of formation in the wilderness, Joshua led the twelve tribes across the Jordan and into battle. After only two military campaigns, the Hebrews had control of the land and were able to settle. For around four hundred years they lived without a centralised government, calling upon judges raised up by God to settle legal disputes and rescue them from trouble as required. Their communal life largely revolved around the law given by God to Moses, and the sacrifices, festivals, rhythms and routines it prescribed, although there were some epic deviations. The phrase 'the Israelites did evil in the sight of the LORD' occurs seven times in the book of Judges, as the Israelites repeatedly adopted pagan practices and worshipped the false gods of the surrounding nations.

During their desert wanderings, the Israelites, under God's detailed instructions, had made a wooden and gold chest known as 'the ark of the Lord's covenant'. It repre-sented God's presence among his people and contained the two stone tablets inscribed with the Ten Commandments, a pot of manna – the food God had provided for them in the desert – and Aaron's rod. Things reached a nadir when the ark was captured by Israel's arch-enemies, the Philistines, and the people decided they needed a king. The first king God gave them was Saul, who made a promising start (once they had pulled him out of his hiding place among the supplies and success-fully got him crowned),[11] but he fell from grace all too soon. Our friend David was the man chosen to take over.

David had grown up in Bethlehem, and spent his boyhood roaming the countryside tending the family flocks. He spent some time in the royal palace playing the harp to calm down the raging moods of Saul, but after his anointing by the prophet Samuel, life didn't change dramatically for him, until he stood before the Israelite army holding the dripping head of the recently slain Goliath. From that moment, we're told, 'Saul kept David with him and did not let him return home to his family'.[12] He's immediately given a style makeover by Jonathan, Saul's son and his closest friend, and soon he's a high-ranking officer in the army. All of a sudden he's plunged into two very distinct sub-cultures within the Israel of the time: first the culture of the royal entourage and second, that of the men united by the bloody battles they fought together. Let's not forget, he was only fifteen years old at this point. I can only imagine how lost and alone he must have felt.

He's gone from obscurity to nationwide fame in dizzyingly short order, and very soon it puts him in danger. A song begins doing the rounds, a catchy refrain comparing David and Saul's Philistine scalp count, and Saul can see where this is headed. The next day, when he and David are hanging out, prophesying and playing the lyre together as they apparently liked to do, Saul tries to pin him to the wall with his spear. Twice.

From here on out, David is not safe in his own home, even when he marries Michal and becomes Saul's son-in-law. Even though Jonathan has his back. Even though the Lord is with him. Saul's mission in life narrows to one sharp goal: to kill David. His days in Saul's service come to an end with a quick escape out of the window, leaving an idol cunningly decorated in goat's hair in his bed as a decoy. It would have been quite a funny prank, if it hadn't been such a dire situation.

This is the second time David has had to adjust to an abrupt cultural transition. Despite his apparent confidence in taking decisive action when needed, the Psalms give us insight into the deep heart-trouble he suffered in private: 'the waters have come up to my neck. I sink in the miry depths, where there is no foothold . . . I am worn out calling for help . . . I am a foreigner to my own family, a stranger to my own mother's children . . . people make sport of me. Those who sit at the gate mock me, and I am the song of drunkards . . . Scorn has broken my heart and has left me helpless.'[13] Yet, in the same psalm, he affirms his secure place in a greater reality: God's love.

Finding ourselves in a culture that is not our own can be a threatening and isolating experience. We might be tempted to do all we can to avoid it, living within a bubble of safe sameness. Perhaps you are British Afro-Caribbean and your food, friends, music and leisure activities are all drawn from those roots. Or you are Welsh and wrapped in a hermetically sealed Welsh life. Or you are middle-class and never rub shoulders with anyone who doesn't speak with Received Pronunciation. All of us, whatever our defining cultural identity, benefit when we step out of our ghettoes and learn from each other. Our cultures will always be our home in some sense, but who wants to stay at home twenty-four/seven?

Shawn and I bought my parents a beautiful polished steel globe as a joint birthday present this year. I'm secretly hoping they will leave it to us in their will, because I love it. I am completely mesmerised by the ability to turn the world on its axis, seeing it so small and contained, east and west, north and south a fluid whole rather than flattened out and defined, limited on a map. Humans have always lived in cultures, and we can't escape that reality – but we also live in God's creation, where 'heaven and earth praise him, the seas and all that move in them'. That was David's comfort. It should be ours.

CHAPTER FOUR
Heartland
My country is my home

Lagos, Algarve

Men love their country not because it is great, but because it is their own.

Seneca

ALTHOUGH AT FIRST I held on to a strong sense of connection to England, after a couple of years of living in Portugal my loyalty shifted. My blonde hair and blue eyes were clear evidence that my genes bore not a trace of Iberian ancestry; I knew only a proportion of the numerous Portuguese tenses and could not sing a *fado* with anything close to authentic misery.[1] I did not even have a Portuguese passport. But none of these impediments barred me from becoming stridently nationalistic. Portugal was my home country, and I loved it, no matter how tenuous my claim to belong.

The country we feel most connected to might well not be the country of our parents, our birth, or even our citizenship. The latest UK census found that there are 7.5 million foreign-born residents living in the United Kingdom. As of 2010, there were 40 million foreign-born residents in the US, while a quarter of the Australian population was born elsewhere. When you choose a country, sometimes your love of that place exceeds that of those who belong to it as an accident of fate. That was my experience.

While my feelings towards Portugal as a country were uncomplicatedly positive, my school experience continued to be a trial. After Samantha unceremoniously dumped me – presumably having found a better way to supplement her lunch – I was entirely friendless. After several terms of agonising isolation, I finally paired up with someone desperate enough to form an association with me. Suzy had a crush on Michael Jackson and would kiss a giant poster of his face before going to sleep each night, and I'd try to appear as if I could relate, because that was the main thing we talked about. Suzy was her mother's only confidante during her father's lurid affair with his secretary, and I in turn was Suzy's only confidante. The cost of having a friend therefore was the loss of a certain degree of innocence.

In addition to the social challenges, the school's approach to academics left a lot to be desired. One among many memorable teachers was a portly Englishman with a baby-pink face and floaty wisps of pure white hair. He may have looked harmless, sweet even, but his approach to science teaching regularly involved total disregard for health or safety. Jars of chemicals would be passed around for us to sniff, no matter how many eight-year-olds fainted, vomited, or went home hallucinating about three-eyed purple rats. On one occasion he set off a 'controlled explosion' in the playground, dramatic enough to cause us to throw ourselves to the ground in terror. And he spent an entire term detailing the practicalities of humanity's future on Mars; all I remember is that it involved something to do with sprinkling wheat seeds into clouds of carbon. Lessons might have been entertaining but were seldom educational in any conventional sense.

When I approached my teens, education began to be a more serious concern and our family had a decision to make: would we all move back to England so us children could go to day schools, or should we stay in Portugal while we went off to boarding school in the UK? I couldn't bear the thought of leaving Portugal, and argued strongly for the latter option. In truth, none of us was ready to say goodbye to our Portuguese life. How my parents were able to put four children through private education on their tiny missionary allowance is another story. My brother's explanation has always been that the whole nature-conservation-charity-founding thing was my father's cover for a lucrative career in the secret service. I prefer to believe they were just really fortunate in their generous friends, and good at digging up trusts whose mandate included supporting those in our exact situation.

We spent the summer before my first term at Dean Close School in Cheltenham crammed into a bronze tin can of a car bombing along the motorways of Britain, visiting family and friends and the various churches that supported A Rocha so far. Wedged between my squabbling siblings on the hot, crisp-covered faux-leather back seat in yet another traffic jam, boarding school awaited like a palace of delights. I couldn't wait.

England seemed strange to us that summer. We had not been back in several years and things had changed. Joey Elliot was able to fill me in on key aspects of popular culture I had missed, although I found it hard to get excited about whether Jason Donovan and Kylie Monogue were an item and was baffled by the trend for non-cyclists to wear cycling shorts. And, although it was still exciting to be reunited, Joey and I were growing up in very different worlds; she had a lot of friends whose every mood she implicitly understood, whereas I was something of a challenge.

Over the course of the summer we enjoyed a huge extended family picnic on the banks of the Thames, ate trifle in a dozen dining rooms, undertook a pilgrimage to my mother's childhood home in Wales and I went to a Christian camp where I prayed earnestly in corners with handsome male youth leaders about my new school. Overall, it was a good two months and I didn't pine for home for a second.

The first day of school finally arrived. We pulled up outside my new address – a gracefully proportioned six-storey building with crumbling pillars and a driveway crammed with vehicles of a whole different species to the tin can. My mum helped me unpack my suitcase into the three-drawer bedside table and made up my bed with my new duvet cover, a shouty purple and black design that I hated even as I chose it on the basis that it might possibly be considered cool. I arranged my Liberty-print photo frame and alarm clock artfully on my shelf, *et voilà* – I was all moved in.

Ten of us slept in the same dormitory. Between us we had parents in Oman, Germany, Indonesia, Korea, Thailand, Saudi Arabia, Wales and Portugal. I don't remember anyone talking about those places though. Our world was the world of the school: boarding house, classrooms, dining room, playing fields. We were marooned in our nasty maroon uniform, an unlikely crew washed up on what was all too far from being a tropical desert island.

After a few days in my new context, the rest of the universe became a blurry concept. I knew on an intellectual level that other places continued to exist, but like Mars or Saturn, anywhere beyond the school grounds felt distant and unreal. I would lie in bed at night and try to bring to mind the dimensions of my room at home and where the low, grey velvet sofa was, and my pinewood desk with its red, bendy-stemmed desk lamp. I'd try to recapture the sound of the rain on the giant eucalyptus that brushed my window and the frogs that sang me to sleep. The images grew paler, however, until they were as faded as an overexposed negative. Along with the loss of a sense of my roots, I lost a sense of myself. I had no idea who I was and there was no one there to remind me.

During the day, I followed my timetabled movements from place to place, disoriented and numb. I learned fast that the Portuguese understanding of how late you can arrive and still be on time did not translate to my new context, where only five minutes early would do. In contrast to the lawless jungle of the international school, here there was a literal book of rules we were expected to memorise and obey. Gum, card games and eating in public were forbidden. Eye contact was mandated. Only ink pens were acceptable for homework, which was now called prep, and if you wanted to go further than about a hundred yards, you had to find someone to go with you.

After the first mufti day (boarding school speak for non-uniform), I balled up my white socks, stuffing them at the back of my drawer, and suffered blisters, because apparently white socks were the very worst crime against fashion. I pretended to like Eurythmics and *Top of the Pops*. I said things were 'lush', and I read a Jilly Cooper novel. This sincere, if resentful, attempt at conformity was not enough, however, and I often found myself alone. The rain started in mid-September and didn't stop, and my school duffle coat went mouldy and lost two toggles. I cried a lot.

In the October half-term I was able to go back home to Portugal and, like a fish that had almost given up thrashing around on the shore, when I was thrown back into water I immediately revived. The weather was still hot enough to spend time on the beach and to take long evening walks around the headland. I gazed with hungry eyes at the red clay soil, the rough bark of the almond trees, the sticky,

ant-covered figs, the scruffy hoopoes and the proud cock-
erels. I sat out on the roof at night and drank in the stars.
I gazed out at the outline of the cliffs of Lagos across the
water, taking in deep, desperate gulps of air that smelled
how it should – not of petrol fumes, rotting foliage and
drizzle. We went out for *bitoques*, garlicky steak with
chips and egg, drank tea under the rubber tree in the
garden, played long games of Monopoly and Risk around
the fire in the evenings. I tried to get it all by heart. I
didn't want to go back and forget it again.

There is nothing like a separation to intensify attachment. Up until that first half-term, I had loved Portugal
somewhat casually. Now I grew passionate. I could have
written ballads about it. This, I decided somewhat belat-
edly, no doubt with a good measure of teenage
melodrama, was the place I felt alive. This was where
I needed to be in order to thrive. Cheltenham was a
monochrome stage in which I couldn't possibly perform
to my potential.

For some time after this revelation, built on the absolute association I made between my motherland and the
boarding school I hated, I became profoundly anti-
England, and would hold forth on the dreadful weather,
the small-minded people, the bland, stodgy food, the
unexciting scenery and the rigid conventionality of
society. Loyalty to one country can easily lead to antag-
onism towards others – an ugly potential feature of
nationalism.

For many of my school friends at that time, the country
where their parents lived was just that: a country where

their parents lived. I suppose it was mostly those who were happy at school who saw things that way. I asked my sister Beth the other day where she tells people she grew up. She said she tells them she lived in Portugal until she was ten and then lived in Bath (where she was at school) until she went to university. After a rocky first year, she loved her time at school. I never felt I lived in Cheltenham, and if it ever comes up in conversation, the most I will ever say is that I went to school there (and then I usually have to add that no, I didn't go to the prestigious Cheltenham Ladies' College, which everyone has heard of). Going to boarding school in England had the effect of making me absolutely sure I did not want it to be my country. *My* country was Portugal.

My divided existence – split between gruelling term-times and blissful holidays – went on for four years, until our time at Cruzinha came to an end and a new chapter began. School got gradually better as I adjusted and came to accept the fact I had to be there, but it didn't endear England to me. I thought of Portugal as my country for a while after we left, and then I thought of myself as a global citizen – with a passport from the UK, but allegiance to no flag.

It would be over a decade until that began to change.

David in Gath

David too spent time away from the land he loved, though not because he was after a better education. After years on the run from Saul, he finally accepted that if he wanted to survive, he needed to leave Israel. He took his six hundred men and his two wives and they settled in Gath.[2] This was a shocking decision, for a number of reasons. Gath was ruled by Achish, king of the Philistines. The Philistines had been Israel's worst enemy for generations, ever since they had been left undefeated in the newly acquired Promised Land.[3] David had come to their attention when he had defeated their champion warrior Goliath as a young boy, with just a sling and some pebbles. He'd won Saul's daughter as a bride, along with a gory collection of two hundred Philistine foreskins, and it was his success against Philistine armies that caused Saul's murderous jealousy – the very reason he had fled Israel. There were songs sung about David and the Philistines, and they were not love songs.

Alone and desperate, David had made an earlier attempt to seek King Achish's protection. But his reputation had preceded him and, quite understandably, he didn't receive a warm welcome. He'd only just managed to escape with his life.

But here he was, eight years later, and for some reason Achish was now willing to take him in. Saul gave up hunting him and, for a year and four months, David and his men dedicated themselves to the Philistine cause. They even got their own town – Ziklag. It must have been a huge relief to the women of the party to finally unpack for longer than a night, to know there would be a next meal and what it was likely to be, to stop moving; even if their resting place was in a strange land, among people they had grown up hating.

What are we to make of David making his home in Philistine territory? How do we reconcile this with the way we would like to think of this anointed future king of Israel? Commentators tend to see this either as one of the many times David messed up, or as a pragmatic and entirely successful strategic move on his journey towards the throne. Either way, God was faithful to David during this sojourn away from home, and his purposes were never under threat.

God's purposes in the Old Testament were intrinsically bound up with the land. According to the theologian Walter Brueggemann, the land is the central theme of biblical faith.[4] To understand how David would have thought about Israel and the role in its history he would ultimately play, therefore, we need to go back to his forefather Abra(ha)m.

When God first spoke to Abram, his name meant 'father', which must have seemed cruelly ironic given his childlessness. God's message to him had two parts. Part two was that he was to become founding father of a nation God would use to bless all the peoples on earth. The new name he was given several years later, Abraham, meant 'father of many', and by then there was nothing cruel about it. Part one, though, was an instruction to leave his home: his country, his people, and his father's household. Abram had grown up in Ur of the Chaldees, and moved as an adult with his wider family to Harran. When the call came to up sticks he was seventy-five years old and well settled.

Sometimes, obedience to God means leaving the place

we are from and heading into unknown territory. The legendary missionary Hudson Taylor sailed for China as a twenty-two-year-old, and would spend fifty-one years there; Eric Liddell, the unlikely Olympic champion whose early life is portrayed in the film *Chariots of Fire*, followed in Hudson Taylor's footsteps a century later; in 1966, after rejections from numerous mission societies, Jackie Pullinger bought a boat ticket for Hong Kong, disembarking with ten dollars in her pocket and no idea how she would get by. All three were responding to a clear call from God and would have a remarkable impact for good in their host nations.

Devotion to a land – that is, a particular country – can easily become idolatrous, in the sense that we want to stay put more than we want to be obedient to God. Examples of people who will go anywhere at the drop of a hat can make us uncomfortable, because they prompt us to ask ourselves if we would do the same. In David's case, remember, there's no suggestion that the move to Gath was anything other than pragmatism; if he was to be king of Israel one day, he needed to stay alive.

The Genesis narrative about Abram is pretty sparse: 'The LORD had said to Abram, "Go . . ." So Abram went' (Genesis 12:1, 4). How did God speak? Was it absolutely clear? No chance that Abram might have imagined it? Did he take any convincing? What was the timeframe between the instruction and when he actually set off? Did he walk around looking at his favourite tree, or sitting on his favourite rock, pocketing a bit of red sand, just to remind him it was real when he was somewhere far away and the dust was yellow? We have no idea. All we know is: God said, and Abram did. He was willing to leave, just like that.

But God wasn't just taking Abram *from* somewhere; he was taking him *to* somewhere, to the 'land I will show you' (Genesis 12:1). It wasn't straightforward – things never are. The land had inhabitants, for starters – the Canaanites. Shortly after Abram and his entourage arrived, there was a famine, and they had to go to Egypt until it passed. When they returned, there wasn't enough pasture for all their animals, and Abram had to part company with his nephew Lot. He continued to live a semi-nomadic existence, living in tents, and the only piece of land he ever technically owned was the field where he buried his wife.

It is impossible to mark the boundaries of the Promised Land on a map. Its parameters are described in different ways in different places in the Old Testament, and they shifted dramatically over time as battles over territory were lost and won. But we know that God gave his people a specific bit of the globe to live on, to settle in and take care of: 'All the land you see I will give to you and your offspring forever . . . Go, walk through the length and breadth of the land, for I am giving it to you' (Genesis 13:15, 18). Under David, the Philistines, Ammonites, Moabites and Amalekites were defeated, and the enlarged boundaries of the land were universally understood to be a sign of God's blessing on David's kingship. Conversely, when the Israelites were unfaithful to God and worshipped idols, the consequence was exile. Between 597 and 539 BC almost the entire population was taken captive: 'By the rivers of Babylon we sat and wept when we remembered Zion . . . How can we sing the songs of the LORD while in a foreign land? If I forget you, Jerusalem, may my right hand forget its skill' (Psalm 137:1, 4–5).

Heartsick for a homeland

Not just in ancient history, but right now, across the world, there are people scattered like dandelion seeds in a gale, far from the soil they grew in and sick with longing to get back. We can decide that such and such a country is our home, and then forces beyond our control might hurl us to a totally different spot on the map. These forces range from slavery and trafficking, to war or ecological disaster, to simply being a child who moves because of a parent's job, or a husband or wife who follows their spouse's work.

One of my daughter's school friends has a Japanese mother, Nami, and an English father. As Nami and I became friends and shared stories, I discovered that although she had not left Japan until her mid-twenties, she had not had a moment's homesickness. The real story of homesickness was her mother's. Nami's mother, Yuko, is Taiwanese, and was engaged to a Taiwanese man when she first met Akira. Akira was a Japanese university student who had come to Taiwan looking for exotic butterflies. There must have been a spark between them, at least attraction, but Yuko was also mindful of the fact that in the post-war world, Japan offered a better life than Taiwan.

When she was twenty, she moved from Taipei to Nagoya, Japan, where she still lives. She has been homesick ever since.

'My mother was never happy,' Nami said. 'She was always complaining about Japan; she couldn't make friends – she felt Japanese people were reserved, and didn't accept her because she was a foreigner. In those days Japan was a very closed society, and she was probably right, but I don't think she tried hard enough.

'She missed the heat, the fruits and food she couldn't get where she lived. She used to say to us, "When you grow up I'll go back to my own country." But now when she goes back, she feels there is no place for her. She belongs nowhere. She has been depressed her whole adult life because she felt she was living in the wrong country. She even used to talk about her ex-fiancé with regret.'

Growing up with a mother who resented the country she lived in had a deep impact on Nami. She felt very unsure of who she was, and lacked the national pride of her 'pure' Japanese friends. It wasn't until she moved to London to study English when she was twenty-six that she realised how deeply she was rooted in Japan – how much she loved the food there, the hot springs in the mountains, the vastly superior medical system. But the country we are from is not always the country we call home. Our feelings of belonging can be transferred, perhaps because of a stretch of time spent elsewhere, or perhaps because our experiences in our country of origin were negative. People fleeing persecution, or economic hardship, or unhappy relationships, are ready and able to embrace a new home country with open arms.

For Nami the transition was slow, but marriage to an Englishman and the birth of her two daughters has made it happen. 'I have lived in England for fourteen years now, and when I go back to Japan I do feel I am going home still. But after two or three weeks I am ready to leave. I don't have independence or control there, and with distance I can see both the good and bad about Japanese culture. I am glad to be raising my children in England, where uniqueness is celebrated and people are encouraged to have an opinion. I want them to understand that they come from two places and that they have a home in both.'

This country and the one to come

Nami loved Japan but was able to live happily in England, loyal to both. She is not fiercely nationalistic and would struggle now to know who to support if Japan ever took on England on the sports field. There are those, however, whose loyalty to their country surpasses that of any other loyalty, who would lay down their lives for their nation without hesitation. Consider the strength of sentiment in the Belgian national anthem: 'O Belgium, dear mother/To you our hearts, to you our arms/To you our blood, O fatherland', or the passion in the Egyptian anthem: 'My homeland, my homeland, my homeland/My love and my heart are for thee.'[5]

Nationalism can have a dark side. While no one would

find a bit of polite flag-waving at a royal wedding particularly sinister, talk about who does or does not belong in a particular country can become nasty. The Nazi party in post-First World War Germany appealed to bruised national pride, and swept people up in an almost religious fervour as it promised to make them part of a nation they could believe in again. History has shown what damage a strident nationalistic ideology can unleash. The history being written today is of the Europe-wide rise of political parties gaining traction with wild statements about past purity and present pollution. As I write, we don't yet know the outcome of the US presidential election,[6] but it has been frightening to observe the support Republican nominee Donald Trump has had for his ideas on how to 'make America great again' – the building of a giant wall along the border with Mexico, the blanket rejection of Muslim visa applications, the rejection of international trade deals benefiting anyone other than the US.

As we in the United Kingdom debated our place in the European Union in 2016, there were moments when public discourse became decidedly ugly. It was as though the topic itself had, for some, legitimised expression of racist sentiment. I heard people on trains, in the street, in pubs and coffee shops talk about 'taking back our country', about 'reclaiming our sovereignty', about 'having a bigger army to defend our rights' and 'keeping out foreigners'. When our common humanity is overshadowed by our disparate national identities, we become vulnerable. One of the many negative emotions I experienced following the news that the UK had voted to leave the European Union was fear;

84

the Union was established primarily in the hope that it would create the best conditions for peace to flourish on the continent. I am afraid of a fragmented future.

Nationalism is concerned not only with who belongs, but also with who doesn't. As people make desperate journeys in search of a safe haven, leaders of wealthy countries fight over who has to take them in. Australian Prime Minister Tony Abbott caused an international outcry with his crackdown on immigration in September 2013; the Australian navy is now instructed to turn away asylum-seekers arriving by sea regardless of circumstance. Closer to home, the photo of the body of three-year-old Syrian Alan Kurdi washed up on a Turkish beach sparked a wave of compassion, but this soon dried up as our focus returned to our own needs and wants. As I write this, French authorities at the port of Calais are forcibly dismantling a camp known as 'the Jungle', where thousands of people have gathered in the hope of making it over the Channel to England. France doesn't want them, and neither do we. It seems no one wants to offer these people a home, even a temporary one. Can prosperous nations realistically be expected to extend an infinite welcome to any who need sanctuary? When, if ever, is it justifiable to pull up the drawbridge so as to protect those inside, at the expense of those outside? I know these questions don't have simple answers; that resources are finite and cultures clash. But I can't help thinking our humanity should trump nationality every time. I picture my own children escaping the UK and arriving as refugees at the Syrian border and try to imagine how it would be for them to be turned away, left stateless, hungry and frightened. At times I have wondered if our whole conception of nationhood is flawed and even at some level wrong.

Even if the idea of nationality is not wrong, it is hard to define what it means beyond the right to live within these (often arbitrarily demarcated) political entities we call countries. There is a short film being shared a lot on social media at the moment about a group of people who volunteered to have their DNA tested, to discern their national origins. We are shown snippets of interviews carried out before the test: confident assertions of roots in Iran, England, Turkey, France; antipathy towards certain other countries. The results are given to the participants in the form of a world map with the countries their DNA reflects circled. Every one of those taking part has strands of multiple nationalities, many from places they had expressed disdain for. One woman says tearfully: 'Everyone should do this. There would be no more war.' Is it time for us to lose the ideal of a home country? Is national sentiment incompatible with kindness and compassion towards suffering fellow humans? Can you love a nation if you also love God?

In actual fact, to love a country, to seek its good and to give it your loyalty is profoundly biblical. The story of the Old Testament is as much as anything the story of a people promised a homeland, gaining that land, losing it, longing to return to it and living in hope because of God's promise that it would be their everlasting possession.

Sometimes it is easier to see things in black and white, and so we set up false dichotomies to give ourselves clarity

– this *or* that. Christians don't have to choose whether to embrace a country as home or wait for a permanent country when the kingdom of God comes in fullness; we must do both. God's words to his people living in exile in Babylon were: 'Build houses and settle down; plant gardens and eat what they produce. Marry and have sons and daughters . . . seek the peace and prosperity of the city to which I have carried you into exile.'[7] They were to put down physical, spiritual and social roots, and get on with the business of living where they were. It was not the land they came from, but they could, and they must, make it home.

The world God has made is physical and specific, and it is in time and space that we encounter him. Paul, speaking in Athens, said, 'From one man he made all the nations, that they should inhabit the whole earth; and he marked out their appointed times in history and the boundaries of their lands. God did this so they would seek him and perhaps reach out for him and find him, though he is not far from any one of us.'[8] Some of us need to become more engaged with national affairs. Not all of us are destined to run for parliament, but we can all be politically literate and use our influence as voters and citizens wisely. We can all work to limit negative impacts on the environment, recycling, improving the energy efficiency of our houses, using public transport when we can. Writing letters to our leaders and to the national press, signing petitions, participating in public consultations, showing up at protests: in societies where free speech is possible, there are multiple ways to have your say and influence the direction of a country. Citizenship confers both privilege and responsibility.

And yet, we must hold our earthly citizenship lightly, because our first allegiance is not to any human authority, but to God. In a sense we are all 'foreigners and strangers . . . longing for a better country – a heavenly one'.[9] We are united with the rest of humanity as the creation of a loving God. We are humans first, and English, American, Japanese, Nigerian, Syrian, Portuguese second.

CHAPTER FIVE

Wanderlust

I have no home

Mkwabene, Zimbabwe

Here today, up and off to somewhere else tomorrow!
Travel, change, interest, excitement! The whole
world before you, and a horizon that's always
changing!

Toad of Toad Hall, *The Wind in the Willows*

GOING AWAY TO boarding school served to turn Cruzinha
into an idyll for me. Each school holiday I re-joined a self
I could live with, in a place that fitted me, among people
who liked me. The intensity of joy this engendered was
compounded by the ever-ticking clock. All too soon we
would be back on the infamous death trap of a road, the

89

EN125, heading for Faro Airport and the next tearful goodbye.

I assumed I would return every holiday, like a boomerang, for as long as boarding school life went on, but while Cruzinha was my idea of paradise, the reality was becoming unsustainable for my parents. My father, in particular, was finding that persevering with the careful study of God's creation alongside the constant threat of its destruction by greedy, short-sighted developers was deeply distressing. And although life in community was rich and varied, as anyone who has experienced it will testify, it can be exhausting – especially so when those you live with have an unchecked passion for ornithology.

As my dad recounts in his book *Kingfisher's Fire*, 'With the huge enthusiasms of different people who joined the team through the eighties and nineties driving us on, the days had been long and the nights of sleep deeply eroded . . . groups were out at night ringing waders on the salinas or catching sea birds at Arabida. Then, of course . . . it made sense to check out the colony of Common Swifts in the abandoned factory at Chinicato, or even worse, to call in at the rubbish dump to look for gulls bearing wing tags or rings from the north. In any quieter moments there was data to enter on the increasingly numerous computers, or help was required to put up equipment for the next day's studies.'[1] The dangers of burnout and exhaustion were real, but there was also a more positive incentive for change: the goal of handing over the project to national leaders was finally achievable. When we'd first arrived, Portuguese Christians with interest and experience in environmental conservation were thin on the ground, but now things were changing.

When my parents began to broach with us children the subject of leaving Cruzinha, our first reaction was outrage. But children don't get to make these decisions, and we gradually absorbed the idea that this unthinkable thing was actually going to happen. For me, it was a case of my mind slowly reshaping around a new idea of the future.

The issue of where to go next became the main topic of mealtime conversation whenever we were at home. Could we explore the north of Portugal? What about Turkey? We'd have to go somewhere hot. Maybe Morocco or Spain? We would clamour to get our suggestions heard, squabbling now and then but in total agreement that we would never, ever move back to England. But despite the airing of all these ideas, by the time we said our final goodbyes to Portugal, all we knew was that we were going. Where to? We had no idea.

A Rocha was now twelve years old and there were increasing signs of interest from people around the world who had caught the vision. With the four of us children in boarding school, Mum and Dad set out on a sabbatical, during which they would visit some of these people and explore the idea of planting A Rocha in other places, as well as taking up invitations from theological colleges who were keen to learn from their thinking and its practical outworking. My siblings and I came to refer to our parents as 'middle-aged travellers', and while we followed the daily round at our respective schools, we did our best to track their movements via printouts of their complex itineraries. This peripatetic existence was to last almost two years.

I was seventeen when we left Portugal, with one more year of school in front of me. Dean Close wasn't home, but neither was it the miserable exile it had been – I had finally made some friends and once I was able to drop Maths and Physics, I loved my studies. During that year we convened as a family in Zimbabwe, Canada and the US; my grandparents' house in Abingdon was our official address. We had a photo album that travelled around with our parents and which we would all pore over when we met, as a kind of keeper of the family identity. In each room she slept in, Mum would drape a colourful cloth over a small table and arrange a few familiar objects – a photo frame, a jewellery box, a perfume bottle. There would always be a corner of a bedroom that felt familiar.

It was strange when it came to finally packing up my sixth-form room at boarding school. While others were loading bags and boxes into their parents' cars for an easy drive home, my stuff was headed for storage in a variety of attics and basements around the country. With hindsight, much of it – if not all – could have gone to the dump, but in this wood between the worlds, I clung to sentimental objects as symbols of belonging: a tatty satin cushion; a plastic snow-globe with – bizarrely – a dolphin inside; smelly sheepskin slippers from the town of Monchique, the closest the Algarve gets to mountains. I wondered when and where I would be able to unpack again.

My friend Nadia works for a homeless charity. She says

she has come to understand that being homeless is about far more than not having an address. It means not having anywhere you can have your stuff around you without having to apologise for it. It means never being able to unpack and arrange your things knowing they will stay where you put them. It is about not being able to see your familiar and meaningful objects arranged on shelves, hanging from the walls, sitting in the cupboards. Even when people are sleeping rough, you can see the powerful urge to make a place that feels like home – a mat laid out in a doorway just so, a decoration of some kind leaned up against the wall, a sentimental object clutched in the hand during sleep.

I had been offered a place at Birmingham University, which I deferred for a year, going to Zimbabwe to teach in a rural primary school with a British charity. All I took to Zimbabwe was one big backpack and one small one. Between them they contained: a thick pair of pyjamas which I knew were totally inappropriate for a hot climate but couldn't bear to leave behind, a couple of outfits, a sleeping bag, a mosquito net, jungle formula insect repellent, a long-wave radio which I lugged around for the entire year without turning it on even once, and a comprehensive first-aid kit. As I boarded the plane with thirty or so other British teenagers, all strangers to me, I had the odd sensation of being untethered from my past. The airport goodbyes had been sad, but once I was off I didn't look back. I had nowhere to miss.

I could have done anything with this newfound freedom, but apparently all I actually wanted to do was get really drunk as often as I could, start smoking and mess around with boys. When I was eleven I'd had an encounter with God – an undeniable, life-altering, terrifying and wonderful experience of his presence, during which he seared his reality and his love onto my heart. It baffles me now that having been touched so personally and profoundly by God, I still thought it would be a good idea to ignore him for a while and do just what I pleased. Anyway, rational or not, that is what I did.

While the charity had seemed, on the face of it, a fairly well-organised outfit with clearly defined objectives, on the ground it comprised little more than a flustered and overstretched coordinator, who put us in pairs and assigned us two Zimbabweans in the same programme, gave us a few days of orientation that consisted of a spotty history of tribal tensions in the area and a handful of useful vocabulary, and then pointed us in the direction of the bus terminal, from which we had to somehow find out how to get to our school postings.

My school was a twenty-minute walk through the bush from Mkwabene, a village two hours from the nearest tarmacked road and made up of a cluster of mud huts, a butchery that sold only fly-encrusted goat, and a bottle store. The school was surprised by the arrival of four youngsters, two of them white and one of them female. They had not known we were coming and they didn't really want us. Nevertheless, they gave us an empty concrete structure to sleep in and allowed us to stay. We discovered that water was to be found by digging into a dry riverbed until it grew wet, a long and dirty process that yielded a gritty, brown liquid very unlike the water that gushes cleanly from taps in more fortunate parts of the world. The toilet was a pit in a shack at the far side of the school grounds. You could smell it at a hundred metres, and getting anywhere near the hole designated for your deposit involved squelching through several inches of vile slime. We used it, though, because the alternative was to crouch in long grass where deadly snakes lurked.

At night we would lie down on the dusty concrete, and try not to think too hard about what might run over our heads. One morning I woke to find myself and everything I owned covered in a thick carpet of flying ants. We had a paraffin stove and discovered you could make a kind of doughy cake from sugar, flour and water. We ate a lot of those, and we drank a lot of beer – it was safer than water, and took the edge off the boredom. As did the cigarettes I'd begun to smoke – a brand called 'Sport' that delivered such a powerful nicotine hit my head would spin after each toxic inhalation.

To begin with we made a half-hearted attempt to get involved in school life. Children walked for miles in bare feet to sit on the ground facing a chipped and scuffed blackboard at the front – no pens or exercise books to be seen. We had no curriculum to guide us, and ended up attempting to lead the children in pointless rounds of 'Heads, Shoulders, Knees and Toes' and 'The Hokey-Cokey'. The final straw for me was when I thought I had struck on a great educational discussion starter and asked the children to tell me about a real-life hero, and why they admired this person. A boy of around ten stood up and, staring coldly into my eyes, told me about his hero, a man he admired for killing white people.

It seemed like a good time to explore southern Africa more widely. I had fallen into a relationship with one of the English boys, Sam, and he and I and a handful of others went on a three-month adventure, travelling the length and breadth of Zimbabwe, down through South Africa to Cape Town, up through Mozambique to Malawi, and from there on a short flight to Kenya.

You think you are invincible when you are young, and we put ourselves in what I now know were rather foolish situations. One time we hitched a lift from a policeman transporting a dead man in a coffin from his village to his place of burial in the nearest city. He pulled over every few miles to knock down a beer or two. By nightfall he was struggling to get back in the car, and it seemed safer to hop out and take our chances in lion country. In Kenya, we decided it would be fun to visit the tiny Islamic island of Lamu. We travelled there in an armed convoy – the route took us through Somalian bandit country, and buses were often targets. There would be no toilet breaks during the seven-hour journey, so I deliberately dehydrated myself rather than risk having an embarrassing accident. In Malawi we swam in the crystal-clear, azure waters of the country's eponymous lake, knowing it was riddled with a nasty disease called bilharzia, which Sam duly contracted.

Along the way we parachuted into other people's lives, coming away with vivid, disjointed impressions that had the surreal ephemerality of dreams. Could I really have sat in bed drinking tea and watching TV with a government official as she discovered she'd been made the Zimbabwean Health Secretary? Was I really brought a jug of Pimm's as I sat sunning myself by a diplomat's pool? Did I play cards all night in a slum dwelling with a family I'd met on a bus? Did I dance on the tables of the workers' bar at the Castle beer factory – and move in with a household of volunteer teachers in Zambia for a week, based on a mutual friend knowing a mutual friend? Did I crawl under a barbed-wire fence in the middle of the night to sit on the edge of Victoria Falls and watch the moon make rainbows in the spray?

I'm almost sure I did.

On one occasion we had a day to kill in Johannesburg before catching the night train to Harare. A group of five of us ended up in a large shopping mall. We wandered into a department store that sold neon orange coats and everyone put one on, paired with huge sunglasses. We split up, roaming zombie-like among the other shoppers, before we were thrown out by angry security guards who didn't understand how funny it was. To me this episode epitomises the facile, superficial nature of the travel we were doing. We were brazenly disrespectful of the places we breezed through on our quest for hilarity and enter-tainment. I burn with shame to think of it. I wanted to think I could make a home wherever I was, but I was more like a bee gathering pollen for my own purposes before buzzing off to the next bright flower.

After three months of travelling we returned to the school, but the frustration of hanging around trying to be useful but knowing we were just in the way grew, and we became resolved to fulfil the terms of our visas, which required us to be doing some kind of charitable work. I had a family friend who lived in Zimbabwe and he organised for me to volunteer in the town of Bulawayo, doing AIDS awareness in secondary schools for the final few months, and Sam and I also found a home for street kids that could use extra hands.

After a couple of months, my relationship with Sam became more than a fling and he began to want to know more about who I was. This involved breaking out of the bubble of the present moment, and it was profoundly uncomfortable. I came clean and told him that deep down I was a committed Christian. He spluttered in disbelief. To him (and he meant this as a high compliment), I was the antithesis of a Christian. We began a discussion which went on for a year, during which we came back from Zimbabwe to the UK – and which ultimately led to our break-up, as I crawled back into God's arms and Sam watched me go, unable to follow me there.

For that year after school, the not-having-a-home thing wasn't a problem. All the people I had gone to Zimbabwe with were at the stage of life where home wasn't quite where their parents lived any more, but they hadn't yet landed anywhere new. We were ready to be off and out of the nest, and happy to be easy-come, easy-go. I thought I had discovered that I didn't need a home in the traditional sense, that I could be a citizen of the world and not worry about a more specific place to belong. Being in my first serious relationship showed me what it was like to belong to a person, and offered me a measure of security. When I came back from Zimbabwe and began shuttling back and forth from university in England to my parents' new home in France, then broke up with Sam, depression and anxiety hit hard. My rootlessness was the best explanation I could find.

Anywhere but here

There is a whole backpacking tribe out there in the world – all sorts of people drifting from place to place, gathering experiences to swap like baseball cards with fellow travellers. I met them in hostels all around southern Africa, in their bleached-out T-shirts, henna-tattooed and peaceably stoned. Some of them had been floating on the currents for years; that footloose, carefree existence can be addictive.

My friends Ali and Jeremy have just come back from a five-month round-the-world trip with their two school-aged children, and they now find themselves wondering how and when they could find a way to repeat what was conceived as a once-in-a-lifetime break from real life. They came over for a barbecue and told us all about it. Their definition of home has changed – it isn't their house any more. In fact, they are really not very excited to be back under their own roof. The revelation that home can be a bed for the night, an unrolled sleeping bag under the stars, a bench on a sleeper train, is heady.

Have you ever been on the London Underground during another washout of a summer day – no sunlight to be seen, fighting the masses for a cubic inch of breathing room in the metal tube taking you to your mundane job in your stuffy little office – and seen one of those sadistic adverts enticing you to buy a package holiday to the mystical land of Anywhere-But-Here? Do you ever have the feeling that if you stay where you are you will miss the life you are supposed to be living, the one where you feel alive every second and the very air hums with potential and tiny exotic birds? Do you ever look at your street, all ordinary and domesticated, and feel utterly disgusted by it?

How are we to interpret these feelings? We might understand them to be a sign that we need to make a change. Perhaps we are just too big for our small town. Perhaps God is calling us to up and move to pastures new. Or it could be that we are beset by *acedia* or *accidie*.

Acedia is an ancient word, used in a monastic setting from around AD 250, and subsequently moving in and out of common usage. Its simple Greek meaning is 'an absence or lack of care' but it is laden with significance – encapsulating apathy, boredom, escapism, restlessness and paralysing despair. Writing in the fourth century AD, the monk Evagrius Ponticus observes, 'The demon of *acedia* – also called the noonday demon – is the one that causes the most serious trouble of all . . . he instils in the heart of the monk a hatred for the place, a hatred for his very life itself.'[2] We have come to be wary of the concept of sin, and who now talks of demons? It is considered heretical to suggest that any of us have responsibility for our mental state; that discipline, work and prayer might be the way to get well. When we feel our commitments chafing, we are encouraged to shake them off, to follow our urges wherever they take us. The American author Kathleen Norris writes, '"Hatred for the place" is a thoroughly modern condition. In a consumer culture we are advised to keep our options open . . . Slamming the door behind us, we head for greener pastures, confident that we are seekers on a holy quest . . . But soon we discover that no place will satisfy us, and no one person, no group of friends, can meet our needs. The oppressive boredom we had hoped to escape is lodged firmly within us.'[3]

There is a temptation to spiritualise restlessness, to diagnose it as some kind of holy calling to a life of pilgrimage. I confess I've fallen prey to that temptation time and time again. Maybe some people *are* supposed to be constantly on the move – there are certainly those who have nomadism in their blood. Christianity wouldn't have spread at the rate it did if Paul hadn't been willing to say goodbye to a settled life. There's a story told in Luke's gospel about a man walking along the road with Jesus, who gets caught up in the moment and makes an impulsive promise: 'I will follow you wherever you go.' Jesus says in reply, 'Foxes have holes and birds have nests, but the Son of Man has no place to lay his head.' You might be forgiven for assuming that means the cost of discipleship is homelessness. For this particular man it would have meant that, and if he had chosen to pay that price to follow Jesus, I'm sure it would have been worth it. But my motivations for resisting the idea of a settled home were mixed at best. I wanted to think I could be at home anywhere, partly because to value a particular place would leave me vulnerable to loss when (I assumed) I would inevitably leave it. But I also thought that fixing to one spot would mean I would live a small, unexciting life, becoming ever more parochial in my outlook.

There's another new word I've discovered lately. This one is German: *Vorfreude.* It means 'the imagined joy of future pleasures'. Living solely for *Vorfreude* is the very opposite of the contentment the New Testament author Paul describes as he writes to the Philippian church from prison, full of good cheer because he's learned to find real joy in the present, regardless of where he is: 'I have learned the secret of being content in any and every situation, whether well fed or hungry, whether living in plenty or in want.'[4]

The American writer Flannery O'Connor said in a 1963 lecture, 'Somewhere is better than anywhere.' Eventually I would come to agree with her, but at nineteen I wasn't there yet, nor anywhere near.

David on the move

There are those of us who have the luxury of autonomy – the ability to choose when and where we move, or whether to stay. But many become nomadic through necessity. Recently I watched the BBC documentary *No Place to Call Home*[5] which tells the heart-breaking stories of homeless people in Barking and Dagenham, where even those in full-time work struggle to afford their rent, and the council has no housing to offer a suicidal teenage girl, or a couple with a two-year-old son. I watched through tears as a dignified South African woman in her late fifties explained how a health issue had led to the loss of her job as a special needs teacher, a subsequent inability to pay for her accommodation and thence to her sleeping in her car. 'I never expected I would have to worry about smelling bad,' she says. 'But now I wonder how to keep clean, and whether I am safe, and how I will find food.' When she's taken in by a temporary shelter in a church, she cries with relief and gratitude, although she's sleeping on a dirty mattress on the floor next to twelve others.

David was homeless for many years, kept constantly on the move as Saul hunted him 'as one hunts a partridge in the mountains' (1 Samuel 26:20). It took him a surprisingly long time to register the fact that Saul really did want him dead – four separate attempts on his life – but eventually he accepted he wasn't safe, and took off. He first sought help from a priest at Nob. The priest was seen giving him bread by the dastardly Doeg, who wasted no time in telling Saul what had happened. The entire town paid with their lives. From Nob, David fled to the country of Gath (the first time around), but they knew of his reputation for slaughtering the enemies of Israel, so he feigned madness and got away. He took shelter in a cave, where he was able to catch his breath, and remained there long enough for word of his whereabouts to reach his family. As soon as he'd fallen out of favour they were at risk, so they joined him, along with a motley crew of the distressed, debt-ridden and discontented. The cave must have been a bit tight for four hundred men with their women and children in tow. They headed for Mizpah in Moab, and David was able to arrange protection for his parents. Quite likely all of them could have stayed but for a prophet named Gad, who said, 'Do not stay in the stronghold. Go into the land of Judah.' We're not told whether this was a message from God or Gad. Part of me wonders if this might have been one of those times when the wires got crossed. There was no obvious purpose behind the ordeal of the subsequent years during which David moved from one hiding place to another, from the forest of Hareth to the hills of Zith, from the desert of En Gedi to the mountains of Maon. But often there is no tidy narrative structure, no discernible meaning to the daily challenges of life. We just have to take it a day at a time (a minute at a time on the bad days), holding on for dear life to the goodness of God.

With psychotic focus Saul pursued his prey, following tip-offs and rumours of sightings with three thousand soldiers and murderous intent – an endless game of hide and seek played on a giant scale. Twice David had the opportunity to kill Saul and put a stop to the madness – the first of which is pretty amusing, if scatological humour is your thing. David and his people were hidden deep inside what must have been an enormous cave, when something, the smell perhaps, alerted them to the fact that Saul was in the cave too, 'relieving himself', shall we say. David's regard for God's anointing of Saul as king was such that he would not have dreamed of laying a finger on him, however perfect the opportunity. He did snip a piece off his robe, however – proof that he had got close enough to have done serious damage but had chosen not to.

For year after year, David had no fixed abode. Finally, he realised he would have no peace until he left Israel altogether, and he headed for Philistine country, where he served the king there, fighting on behalf of his lifelong enemies. When Saul died, finally, David was swiftly anointed king of Judah, and made his home in Hebron for seven and a half years.

David didn't keep a diary during his wilderness years, or not one that we know of. But he did write psalms. He wrote Psalm 34 while hiding in Gath, facing danger from the Philistines as well as Saul, testifying that 'those who seek the LORD lack no good thing'.[6] Psalm 57 was written in a cave. I imagine he was filthy, dog-tired, ravenously hungry, not to mention emotionally overwrought. I would have fallen apart at the seams after just one day of playing the fox to the hunt, and David endured years of it. The psalm refers to his troubles but most of it consists of confident assertions of God's love, faithfulness, glory. David's 'heart is steadfast'.[7] Psalm 63 was composed in the Desert of Judah. In a land with no water, he thirsts for God, 'because your love is better than life'.[8]

It is comforting to know that so much of what advertisers, psychologists and our own assumptions tell us we need in order to be content can be stripped away, and to discover that in fact we survive just fine. Nonetheless, for me those two years of homelessness left a less healthy legacy. They left me battling the demon of *acedia* that whispered to me I would never be content, that I would never belong, that I was condemned to live out my days with a persistent sense of restless dissatisfaction. Battling this demon would take me on a journey that involved no changes of scenery, no planes or trains, no backpacks and no passport. As I was discovering, wherever you go, there you are. I needed to find a home inside myself.

CHAPTER SIX
The anchored soul
At home in myself

Moulin de Daudet, Fontvieille, France

If we know ourselves, we're always home. Anywhere.
Glenda, the good witch of the north,
The Wizard of Oz

IN MARCH 2011, Nadine Schweigert, a thirty-six-year-old single mother of two from North Dakota, put on a silky teal gown and married herself in a ceremony attended by forty family members, friends and well-wishers. In an interview with the *Huffington Post*, she stated, 'I feel very empowered, very happy, very joyous.'

Ms Schweigert may have taken the concept of self-love to a batty extreme, but behind the oddity of the situation

107

is someone wanting to say to the world that she's at home in herself. Having survived a divorce, lost fifty pounds and rebuilt her shredded self-esteem, she now chooses to cherish herself, even dressing up and going out on solo dates. While I wouldn't go as far as a public ceremony to make the point, I do feel very strongly that if we are not first at home in ourselves, we will never be at home anywhere.

My friend Erika grew up in South Africa. She and I became friends when we overlapped for a year in Surbiton. We've only known each other a few years, but from the first time we met I was drawn to her peacefulness and aura of stability. We have talked a lot about what home means to us, but the last time I stayed with her where she now lives, in a village outside Luton, I pushed her for a definition, thinking she was someone who would say her sense of home came from her marriage. She and her husband Jonas have an extraordinary closeness, a relationship of rare harmony and mutual respect. So I was surprised when she said without hesitation that her home was within herself, and as a result of that conversation I asked her if she would allow me to include her story here.

Erika's understanding of home was shaped by a number of key events. When she was three, her mother developed an aggressive form of Hodgkin's lymphoma. 'I remember when and where I was when I realised it wasn't flu,' she said; 'that she was destined to die. She would have died, but she was prayed for and there was a miracle. The doctors couldn't explain it and they made her go through all the treatment anyway. So there was a stretch of about two years when I lived with my maternal grandparents, and my sister lived with the other grandparents, and I felt like I had two homes. When my mum was cleared, we moved house, into a beautiful, huge, light-filled place with a massive swimming pool and these gorgeous gardens that went on forever. I always pictured myself getting married in the gardens.

'After apartheid ended, the government introduced a programme called Black Economic Empowerment. My father had a business publishing textbooks for schools, and all his contracts were given to black people. He lost his income, his house and his marriage. I was twenty-one by the time they had to let the house go, but it hit me hard. I even had therapy about it!

'At that point I'd been living in Holland for a year, working as an au pair and trying to figure out a direction for my life. My grandparents were Dutch, so there was a lot that was home-like in Holland. When I came back and my childhood house had been sold, I felt like I didn't have a base. But I found my vocation in psychology and I met Jonas, and those things gave me a new sense of grounded-ness. When we were first married, we lived in Jonas's house, which was full of his family's furniture, so that wasn't ideal. It felt like his space. After we'd been married for three years, we moved to England, and we've been here eleven years now. Both our kids were born here. There have been four houses, but where we are now is our favourite.'

What I wanted to know, though, was when, amidst all that upheaval, she began to locate her understanding of home in herself. It made sense to me that she's found a way to be at home in herself, partly because I've been a recipient of the hospitality she offers, a welcome into who she is and the gift of her presence. 'The first time I thought of home that way I was only nine. We had big school exams that lasted a week, and we'd been assigned a desk for that time. I remember looking around my place, and trying to settle into it, trying to be at home there. It wasn't the desk I'd wanted to be at; I wanted to be in the corner by the radiator. So I realised I had to make home in myself.'

Is being at home in yourself the same thing as self-love, I asked? 'I don't think so,' she said thoughtfully. 'There are always things we need to work on, that we struggle with and maybe shouldn't accept. Like, I don't accept that I don't do any exercise – I need to change that. But there's a settledness that comes from accepting the reality of who we are right now, the good and the bad, and living out of that. And sometimes when we start thinking we want to move house, and we go on lots of property websites fantasising about what a perfect house will do for us, we actually just need to deal with something internally.' They were wise words, and a timely reminder. Property websites aren't my thing, but I had been looking at job ads a lot recently and I felt suddenly sure it wasn't a new job I needed, but some work on my insides.

Who am I?

Erika is someone with an anchored soul; she has explored her 'interior castle',[1] accepted and chosen to love what she's found there, while remaining committed to ongoing renovation and restoration. How many of us can claim to have fully moved in, taken proud possession of who we are? For me this is definitely more aspiration than reality. Self-acceptance involves a daily choice to override our harsh inner critic and the unkind voices from our past. It means seeing and understanding how we are wired, our strengths and our frailties, the quirks that make us unique.

It has taken me a long time to settle into being myself. The eight years I spent at the international school in Portugal, being told day after day that I was ugly, unacceptable, odd, contemptible and boring, took their toll. I came to believe those things were true, and I rejected myself just as my classmates had. In my first year at boarding school, when I found myself ostracised and bullied, it was all the confirmation I needed that I was indeed unacceptable. I was not able to hear or receive the counter-messages of affirmation that came from the people – and I see now that there were many of them – who loved me. In piecing together a picture of who we are, we naturally look at the way we are seen by others. That's not necessarily a bad thing, but it can't be our only source of self-knowledge. The scary thing is how, if we are not hyper-vigilant, we can become what we are told we are. Anyone who has been in an abusive relationship knows how constant criticism can reshape a personality. Anyone who has spent time working under a difficult boss, or who has been pulled into the orbit of an overbearing would-be friend, or has had to rub shoulders on a regular basis with someone who clearly doesn't like them, knows how hard it is to resist being reshaped in the image of how you are seen. I have no easy solution for this problem, but I've learned that I don't have to accept the labels so liberally handed out by one and all. And I've made my peace with the idea that different people will bring out different sides to my personality, which doesn't mean I have no intrinsic self.

The bullying at school has had a lot to do with my struggle to accept myself, but a far more significant factor has been depression.[2] I first encountered what some call 'the black dog' and what I referred to as 'the dragons' soon after I started at Dean Close. In the early 1990s there was far less awareness of mental-health issues among teens – or anyone, come to that – and it took several years before I had a medical name for the dragons. From the age of thirteen until my early twenties I had frequent bouts of major depression combined with anxiety, and long stretches of dysthymia – low-grade, chronic depression. One of the many ways depression sucks, and it sucks in a great many ways, is the way it alienates you from yourself. You become a person you don't recognise – a shadow self, a self that tortures you with negativity, hopelessness, confusion and a leaden exhaustion – and you never get a break, because that awful person is you.

Depression came and went during school. In between lows, I embarked on some pretty standard teenage navel-gazing in my quest to discover who I might turn out to be. There were clues: in our school it was traditional for the students to produce a yearbook after we'd finished doing our GCSE exams at sixteen. There was a list of awards based on a vote – 'Most likely to get a life sentence', 'Best legs', 'Future dictator', and so on. I was disproportionately thrilled to be voted, by a massive majority, 'Most eccentric' and 'Best sense of humour'. These were qualities I could work with. These were labels that didn't hurt.

Other clues about the essence of my nature were to be found in the weekly letters from my mother. She'd intersperse these chatty missives about goings-on at Cruzinha with confident assertions about my qualities: she seemed sure I was and always had been brave, interesting, bright and good at friendship, despite all current evidence to the contrary. While part of me thought, 'Well, she's my mother, of course she's going to think I'm OK,' another part of me carefully filed her observations under the category of 'Facts about what I'm like'.

When I think now about how I tried to construct a sense of self like a papier-mâché sculpture, papering over the self I couldn't live with as best I could, it all seems very fragile and contrived. But I'm learning to be kind, to myself as well as others, and I know that at that time, this was the only way I knew to be me.

My year of adventures after leaving school showed me a different direction I could take as a person, should I choose. I was freer than ever before from the exhausting task of making others like me, but conversely selfish and insensitive. I knew I could make people laugh, but when I did so it was often by making cruel observations about both strangers and friends. I was spontaneous and unpredictable, and therefore unreliable. By the time I came back to Europe, though, I knew the kind of person I wanted to be, and I was ready to put in the work to become her.

Birmingham is a great university in a great city and my degree was in English Literature and African Studies, not the most intensive fields of study. My schedule allowed me masses of time to make friends, join committees, get involved in the Christian Union, go out dancing and sit around chewing over the meaning of life with friends, while eating questionable curry. I'd had a reprieve from depression on my travels, but even with so much to be grateful for and distracted by, it hit me again around halfway through my first term, mildly enough that I could hide it that time, and then again with force at the start of my second year. Three friends and I had moved into a tiny redbrick terrace in Selly Oak, a short distance off campus. After just a few weeks happily playing house together, they were unexpectedly confronted with a new housemate: Depressed Jo. I still had no name for this thing that took me over, but Rachel was studying psychology and she brought me her textbook one day and read out the bit about depression. Every word matched precisely how I was feeling. Armed with this new information, but needing confirmation even if a little afraid about the implications of a clinical diagnosis, I went to stay with Mo, a close family friend and, more pertinently, a psychiatrist. I sat blubbing on her bright blue sofa, explaining as well as I could the way the walls closed in on me, gravity failed, everything had sharp edges that hurt me, how my thoughts wrapped me up in chains, how I had to hold on to the railings when I walked to classes because I so badly wanted to step in front of a bus and end the nightmare. She listened kindly, nodding and handing me tissues now and then. And when I dried up, she said I had depression and told me the treatments available.

There are all sorts of not very good reasons why I waited over two years to act on her advice. I didn't want to admit I couldn't deal with it on my own – I thought it would make me seem more weak and broken than I already was. I didn't believe talking about problems could possibly make them go away. I didn't want to take medication because I thought that would make me officially mad, and that it would turn me into a zombie who didn't feel the bad things but who would miss out on the good things too. I thought I was a person who had to suffer the lows for the technicolour glory of the highs. So I thanked Mo for giving me her diagnosis, and off I went.

The issue of where to go and what to do after graduation was solved one day over lunch, at our new home in France, a whole year ahead of time. I was home for the summer holidays; Dad was opening the post, and it included a bundle of information about a course he and Mum were going to be teaching at Regent College. He looked up with a gleam in his eye and said, 'You should come with us.' What he had in mind was a summer school, but as I looked over the brochure, fireworks began going off in my head and suddenly all I wanted to do was move to Vancouver and get a Masters.

So, after my last year at Birmingham, off I went. It was another major transition, and while I was convinced it was the right thing to do and the right place to be, I soon hit rough inner terrain and found I was feeling pretty low. My internal narrative about my depression held that it stemmed from all the moving around. It made perfect sense that it would hit at this juncture, therefore, and I was ready for it, I thought – braced to ride it out as I'd done so many times before. I was living in a large, light, wooden house with a sofa on the front porch, a fireplace in the front room, and enough beds for seven of us, with floor space for more as and when required. I slept in a bottom bunk; Marcy, a fellow-student from Victoria, slept on the top bunk. My six 'roomies' set about teaching me to speak Canadian, inducted me into West Coast life and generally made me feel welcome – but I felt unsettled, and then unhappy, and then depressed.

I'm convinced my established cycle in and out of depression would be ongoing even now, if it hadn't been for a conversation I had one dark December afternoon with Thena, the Dean at Regent. She'd given me a lift home from 'school' (it took me a while to get used to the North American definition of the word, applied to anywhere you can learn things), and we parked so as to keep talking when she picked up that I was struggling.

'You should see my friend Judith,' she said. 'She's a fabulous psychiatrist—'

'Stop right there,' I interrupted. 'I don't need a psychiatrist. I'm managing just fine. I always come out of these patches eventually, and I'm not nearly as mentally ill as other mentally ill people.'

She picked up my hand and, holding it, said very gently,

'A person can live their whole life with one arm in a sling. But think how much easier it would be to have two arms to do things with. Let me talk to Judith and see if she can fit you in, just for an initial chat.' By the time I got out of the car I'd agreed.

Doctors must get so frustrated when patients come to their appointments with their own diagnosis set in stone. During my first session with Judith I told her I was depressed because I had moved around so many times that I didn't know where I belonged. By the end of the hour, Judith had disabused me of that theory. 'You are not unsettled because of the moving, at least not in a funda mental sense,' she said. 'What we need to work on together is finding a way for you to integrate your feelings and experiences – the positive and the negative. What you identify as a feeling of unsettledness comes from a fragmented self, where anger and sadness are seen as dangerous – emotions to be feared, even denied.' Judith and I ended up working together on this fractured self for three years and, by our last session, I could see I had made some progress.

Open house

My fear that a quest for inner peace and self-acceptance was indulgent and an unworthy use of time and energy persisted session after session, until one day Judith put it so clearly and compellingly I finally got it. 'Feeling happy with ourselves is not an end in itself,' she said patiently, after I'd raised it yet again, using it as a reason to quit. 'It is the fruit of living our true identity as God's cared-for people. Of course it is an endless process of healing from wounds that have damaged our sense of well-being and letting go of the anxieties that keep us double-checking our pulse and looking in the mirror. But our striving is not towards self and feeling good but towards living our true identity.'

I believe a central truth of identity is that we are God's beloved. And this is not a long-distance love affair: mind-blowingly, the Bible speaks about God himself making his home in us, as Eugene Peterson expressed John 1:14 in *The Message*, 'The Word became flesh and blood, and moved into the neighborhood.' The Word – Jesus – lived in the neighborhood for thirty-three years, and then began to prepare his friends for a hard goodbye. Over the Passover supper, just a few hours before his arrest, he told them he had to leave, but then came the good news: the Spirit, God's spirit, would live with them and – more than that – would be in them. 'Anyone who loves me will obey my teaching,' he said. 'My Father will love them, and we will come to them and make our home with them.' God makes his home with us, if we let him. If God himself is willing to dwell in us, we have every reason to be confident of our intrinsic worth. Of course, 'asking God into your heart', as the saying goes, is not the end of low self-esteem, as Exhibit A (that's me) incontrovertibly demonstrates. The Holy Spirit overpowered me with love as an eleven-year-old that time on the beach, yet as a thirty-eight-year-old I still have moments of crippling self-doubt. But I try to remind myself that I am the handiwork of a divine creator whose stamp of approval carries far more weight than an appraisal from anyone else – including me.

Psalm 139 is a beautiful glimpse into the underpinnings of David's self-acceptance. David stands before God in the full knowledge that he is *seen*: his actions, his thoughts and his words are laid bare. There's no hiding. At some level we must understand that the very idea of concealing any part of who we are from God is absurd, but ever since Adam and Eve lurked behind the trees in the Garden of Eden in their natty fig-leaf outfits, hoping God wouldn't find them, we've tried to keep our mistakes in the dark. How foolish we are. As David writes, 'If I say, "Surely the darkness will hide me and the light become night around me," even the darkness will not be dark to you: the night will shine like the day.'[3] David was far from perfect and had plenty he might have liked to keep under wraps, but we don't get the sense from this psalm that total exposure before God is unbearable or dangerous. For David, God's hand upon him is wonderful; God's inescapable presence is comforting. He has total confidence that who he is and what he's done won't cause God to reject him.

David had developed an impervious sense of worth, grounded in his understanding of himself as created, known and loved by God; but he knew there was work to be done. Psalm 139 ends with his plea that God would test him and search him for anxious thoughts and offensive ways. He's a work in progress, but God is leading him 'in the way everlasting'. The self that God has made each of us to be is here for the long haul. Whether we choose to love it as God does, or not, it is the home we've been given, and there's no moving out.

In some regards I am a very slow learner, and another lesson that it's taken a long time to get my head around is that self-love and the ability to love others are inseparable. Only when I am at home in myself can I offer true, from-the-heart hospitality to others. The writer and researcher Brené Brown, best known for her TED talk on vulnerability,[4] spent many years studying human connection, identifying the characteristics of those who are able to form strong bonds with others. She concluded that to connect we must believe at some level that we are worthy of love. Her message is: 'You're imperfect, and you're wired for struggle, but you are worthy of love and belonging.' Jesus' command to love others as we love ourselves, after all, presupposes self-love. The self-love part is not commanded – it is assumed.

Sadly, we don't always love ourselves well, and when we don't it generally means we don't love others well either.

The embodied self

Being at home in ourselves means as much as anything being at home in our bodies. Our bone, muscle, fat and blood are not incidental packaging. But current societal pressures mean it is harder and harder to live happily in our skin. In a survey in 2014 by *Glamour* magazine in the USA, 80 per cent of respondents said just looking at themselves in the mirror made them feel bad. Plastic surgery, punishing exercise regimes, strange powdered food substitutes – these are *de rigueur* in a culture that idolises youth and a slender frame. It is hard in this toxic environment to love our bodies, to embrace our physicality as it is. We might be tempted instead to focus on an idea of ourselves as an ephemeral soul, to disassociate from our flat feet, sallow complexion and weak chin and instead focus on our inner beauty.

In her wonderful book *Body*, subtitled 'Biblical spirituality for the whole person', Paula Gooder writes, 'The tendency to focus on the soul at the expense of the body is one of the reasons why the Christian tradition has had such an ambivalent relationship with the body throughout its history.'[5] She argues that the idea of the physical body being a temporary and 'non-spiritual' husk, to be discarded on our deathbeds, originates in the philosophy of Plato, and not in the Bible. Paula and I have become friends lately and I've had the opportunity to chew her ear off with my thoughts and questions about her understanding of Paul's teaching on bodies and their long-term prospects. (Paula is a Pauline scholar, as you'll soon find out if you meet her!) She doesn't think Paul teaches that there is a soul or spirit that exists separately from the body. In other words, soul, spirit and flesh are indivisible. Eternal life means eternal life as bodies, and more than that, as *these* bodies.

When I asked her to help me understand how that could possibly work when we start to decay almost from the moment of birth (and quite visibly once you get to my age, I'm forced to admit), she reminded me of the seed metaphor in 1 Corinthians. A seed is packed with the full potential of the tree it is to become, even though it looks nothing like it. We talked about whether there would be people of different ages in heaven, my primary concern being that I'd be landed with looking after a bunch of rowdy toddlers world without end. 'How I imagine it,' she said, 'is that all of us will be who we were at every age, and who we were meant to be: our full selves. There's real comfort there for anyone who's lost a baby. I think they'll get to meet the full person – everything that baby could have been.' I love that idea, and while I know we can only grasp through mists of mystery far beyond our ability to understand, Paul's teaching and Paula's inter-pretation sit well with me.

So who am I? What is the self that I must embrace and make my home? I am this body, I am this mind, this personality, this character. I am a flawed and imperfect and broken person, created and beloved by God. And before I can be at home anywhere or with anyone, I must be at home in me.

CHAPTER SEVEN

'Til death
My marriage is my home

Love, you are my hermitage,
My dwelling for ever.
Here have I built my home,
Here in you alone.[1]

Mike Mason, *The Mystery of Marriage*

IDLING AWAY TIME on Facebook the other day, I clicked on a link to a short film several people had shared on their timelines, simply called 'Chloe'. The film begins with a man, Walt, describing how at ten years old he'd had a vision of himself as a grown man, swinging a laughing little girl with olive skin and dark eyes around by the arms in his parents' back yard, and felt God say to him, 'This is going to be your daughter, and her name is going to be Chloe.' Meanwhile, Annie was a few years behind him, growing up across the pasture and admiring him as the kind of boy she'd like to marry one day.

When she went to university, he lived nearby and they began to date. On one of their first dates, they talked about their dreams and hopes for the future. Annie told Walt that more than anything else, she felt God had made her to be a mother, and she'd already got a name picked out: Chloe. They were floored by the coincidence, but Annie was fair skinned and blue eyed. No child of theirs would look like the girl in the vision. Walt had no idea what to make of it all.

Telling the story years later, Annie says, 'I think we both knew pretty early on that we were going to get married. The best way I can describe it is that Walt felt like home to me, from the very beginning. I felt like, "Yes, this is where I belong, with this guy."' As she speaks, footage from their wedding plays – the two of them a blazing bonfire of pure and hopeful love. They've found their home: you can see it in their eyes; you can hear it in the spontaneous, laughing applause of their gathered friends and family.

This film is not primarily about Walt and Annie's marriage, however, but the painful years of infertility, doubt and depression that threatened to split them apart. The glorious wedding day, all that certainty and delight in each other, all that was concrete poured into foundations that would need to hold strong in order for the 'house of them' to withstand what was coming. There's a great twist, but I'm not going to spoil it for you. You'll have to go and watch it yourself.[2]

When I think about marriage as home, I think about people who feel safe and accepted by one another, but I also think about a promise that holds them together, that is bigger than them and bigger than anything life can throw their way. I want to believe that at its best, marriage is a fortress, a port in a storm, an anchor in the ocean.

Unholy matrimony

It is important to me to talk about marriage as home, because I've found there to be something powerfully grounding about a lifelong commitment to another person with whom you share life and find continuity regardless of changing context. In a very tangible sense, Shawn is my home. But I know this definition of home may be painful for some – for the divorced or bereaved, for the unhappily married, for the single person who longs to be half of a couple. Just as a strong marriage can give a feeling of 'at-home-ness', so a difficult marriage or single-ness can make people feel homeless.

My friend Paula had a short-lived first marriage in her early twenties. She told me more about it recently, still finding it hard to revisit nearly two decades later.

'Glenn and I were at school together. I've no idea why I married him really, except that my dad had died and I was looking for some kind of stability. I remember on our wedding day, posing for pictures in the entrance to the church. There was a wasp buzzing around us, and Glenn panicked and began swatting at it. I looked at him and I thought, "You are so irritating," and right then I wondered what I'd done.

'I'd known he had a gambling problem when we got together but I thought it would somehow all work out. We'd go to the pub, and if I went to the toilet he'd be red and sweaty when I came back. He'd have run over to play on the fruit machines. He'd lie about it but then eventually confess and we'd have a huge row. I couldn't believe anything he said – there was no trust or safety in our relationship at all.

'Really soon I wasn't sure how I'd get to the end of a week with him, let alone the end of my life. I felt so trapped, and I hated going home. It was terrifying – we lived in the same house but he felt like an intruder. It wasn't just that he was in my physical space – it was that I wasn't at home with him. I can understand how people can run away from their lives – just walk out one day and not come back.

'I was a local reporter, and was offered a job on a national paper. It meant I'd be away a lot. Glenn told me to go for it because he was excited about the money. But then a friend of his came over and said, "I don't know how you put up with it, mate." And because of that he changed his mind about me taking the job. He was totally spineless.

'We were only married for a year. I went off to Edinburgh

with a friend, and never went home. It turned out he was in a relationship with someone from his work.'

A few years later, Paula met someone new; they have been married for thirteen years now, and have three children. The love and respect between them is evident, and although they have their struggles, as all couples do, their relationship is solid and secure.

Back in 'ye olden days', romantic love was not the primary reason for getting married. Other considerations held sway, such as the formation of strategic alliances, or the pursuit of status, wealth and security. But the idea that Shakespeare invented romantic love is nonsense. Song of Songs, written well over a thousand years ago, contains some of the most passionate poetry ever penned:

Place me like a seal over your heart,
like a seal on your arm;
for love is as strong as death,
its jealousy unyielding as the grave.
It burns like blazing fire,
like a mighty flame.
Many waters cannot quench love;
Rivers cannot sweep it away.[3]

Tradition holds that Song of Songs was written by David's son, Solomon, but I don't think David would have resonated with the idea of finding home in a marriage. If marriage is a house, David was a real-estate mogul with a large and varied portfolio. He gained new property on

a whim, took little care of it, and died in a rented apartment. David's life was full of wild contradictions – he was
a good friend and a horrible husband; a worshipper and
a sinner; a bloodthirsty soldier with a violent temper,
and a man of peace who spared his enemy's life over and
over again. We've been tracking with him as we've
explored each dimension of home, but at this juncture
he's not much of a help. As I was wondering whether to
ditch him, albeit temporarily, it struck me that perhaps
his rocky marital record could be a good counterpoint to
any idealised picture we might be tempted to conjure up.
And it would be a shame to skip over what turns out to
be quite a colourful aspect of his story.

Where God was concerned, David was mostly passionate,
loyal and committed; but against the backdrop of a grand
divine romance came a parade of women, some of whom
are not even named in the biblical narrative. Perhaps even
David had trouble keeping track of all those names. I can
almost picture him sitting down to supper and saying,
'Hey, Machishag . . . Abigoam . . . Hagg-face-what's-your-
name – could you pass the salt?'

David's first wife was Michal, Saul's daughter. When
Saul discovered this poor girl had feelings for the man
he hated and feared more than anyone, he was delighted:
'I will give her to him so that she may be a snare to him
and so that the hand of the Philistines may be against
him.'[4] Lovely. David's calculating approach to the lovelorn
girl was no better than her father's: for him, the relationship was about becoming the king's son-in-law, and once
he was convinced this was a good idea, he happily acquired

the necessary foreskins for the bride-price, and a few more for good measure. David and Michal didn't have long to settle into life as newlyweds before David's murderous new father-in-law became too much of a threat to ignore and, once he'd gone, Michal, who we are twice told was in love with David, and who had saved his life at great personal cost, was swiftly dispatched to marry Paltiel of Gallim, about whom more later.

David went off without a backward glance and quickly picked up a new wife, Ahinoam of Jezreel. Ahinoam was joined by Abigail. Polygamy is not uncommon in the Old Testament and God seems (surprisingly) silent on the issue, but I don't think we can take that as implied approval. My own understanding is that God may have allowed it as the best way of caring for vulnerable women in that particular time and place. Brutal and almost constant warfare meant fatalities among men were extremely high, and without a man for protection and provision, women in the ancient Near East were vulnerable to slavery, prostitution and destitution. A polygamous marriage was not ideal for any of the parties involved, but it solved a particular problem.

Abigail's story is certainly an intriguing one. She was married to a prize buffoon, Nabal, and saved David from entering a petty but bloody dispute with him by reminding him of his true identity: 'When the Lord has fulfilled for my lord every good thing he promised concerning him and has appointed him ruler over Israel, my lord will not have on his conscience the staggering burden of needless bloodshed.'[5] When Nabal died, struck down by God ten days later, David sent for Abigail – not insensible to her beauty, I suspect.[6] These two wives stayed with him in the wilderness, and he apparently became quite attached to them. When they were stolen from Ziklag by an Amalekite raiding party, he wept copious tears and set off immediately to get them back. Could it be that these two gave him a sense of home during a time of great instability and constant change? We can only speculate.

Once Saul had died and David had been anointed king of Judah, he settled in Hebron, where he added a few more wives into the mix: Maakah, Haggith, Abital and Eglah. By now he was making a mockery of God's design for marriage – two becoming one flesh, as we read in Genesis, cleaving to one another in lifelong fidelity. What did marriage mean to him, I wonder? Was it anything beyond political manoeuvring, sex on tap and a means of producing plenty of empire-securing sons (not that that worked out so well)? And what would it have been like to be one of the wives? David was still young, in good physical shape, and easy on the eye. He was on an upward trajectory, gaining prestige, respect and territory all the time. We know from his psalms that he was passionate and emotional, that he loved God and wanted to please him, and also that he appreciated the good things in life. To have been David's only wife, valued and beloved, would have been a fine thing. To have been one among many women to share his attention and his bed must surely have been a nightmare.

With David established as king and living in Hebron, Michal re-enters the story. She'd been married to Paltiel for over a decade, but her loss rankled with David – it somehow represented all the injustices he had suffered from Saul; plus, he'd paid for her with a pile of foreskins and in his mind she was rightfully his. With Saul dead and his son Ish-Bosheth the weak and ineffective leader of Israel,[7] David struck a deal with the commander of Israel's army and got Michal back. We don't know what Michal's thoughts or feelings were about the situation, but Paltiel was devastated, walking and weeping behind his stolen wife until he was told to go home. Michal effectively exchanged a husband who loved her shamelessly and wholeheartedly for one who, as I read it, had never loved her and never would.

When David was thirty he became king over Israel as well as Judah and made Jerusalem the capital city of both. In Jerusalem, we're told, he took more concubines and wives, but we're not given names or numbers. There is one other woman who plays a significant part in David's story, though, and if David's track record with women so far hasn't endeared him to you, this next bit is only going to make things worse. It was usual for kings to lead their armies onto the battlefield, but for some reason David chose to send his soldiers to fight without him on this occasion. While his men were off fighting the Ammonites, Israel's Enemy Number One, David was poncing around his palace with time on his hands. While walking around on his roof terrace one evening, he spotted a naked woman. Given how many naked women he had access to at any one time, we can assume this one must have been pretty spectacular in order to catch his attention.

He got someone to find out who she was, and then, in full knowledge that she was married, with her husband off fighting his wars, David had her delivered to him – and then sent home. When he discovered she was pregnant, David thought it would be a good idea to pass the baby off as her husband's, so he had him brought home from war on a spurious excuse, and gave them time for a quick conjugal. Uriah the Hittite, unfortunately for David, was too honourable to indulge in nookie when his fellow soldiers were sweating it out on the battlefield, so when that plan didn't work, David ordered him to be sent to the front line, instructing the army commander to send him out in front so he would be sure to be killed. Problem solved – finally. After her official period of mourning, David had Bathsheba brought back to the palace and made her his wife.

It is an ugly episode, and perhaps, like me, you are tempted to read it from a moral high horse. But we need to dismount, lay down our judgement, and prostrate ourselves with David before a holy God. Who among us has not objectified, abused, controlled, demeaned another person? Who can say they have not repeatedly attempted to steal God's limelight? Which of us does not get things wrong, in ways large and small, on an hourly basis? God's great metaphor for his relationship with humankind is that of a marriage in which only one person keeps faith with the covenant. We are unwilling, unable to stay true. David's failure here was spectacular, and the consequences would be severe. But as Eugene Peterson puts it, 'David's sin, enormous as it was, was wildly outdone by God's grace. David's sin cannot, must not, be minimized, but it's minuscule compared to God's salvation from it.'[8] Sin is a given. The real problem is when we refuse to recognise it for what it is.

David's recognition came via a story, a story in which a rich man stole the only, precious ewe lamb of a poor man. It took his priest, Nathan, to spell out the meaning of the tale and David's role in it, but once David was confronted with the true picture of what he'd done, he was distraught. His words in Psalm 51 bleed regret: 'You are right in your verdict and justified when you judge . . . My sacrifice, O God, is a broken spirit; a broken and contrite heart you, God, will not despise.'

David died in the arms of a woman, not a wife or even a concubine, but a young and beautiful virgin with the unenviable job of keeping the shivery old man warm as he inched towards death. David had many ways of understanding home, but I'd hazard marriage wasn't one of them. I found a home in marriage, though, and this is how it happened.

The course of love

When I told you about how my move to Canada came about, I omitted part of the story. While I was still fragile with depression, in my second year of university, I'd met someone who wanted to 'fix' me.

From my earliest childhood I dreamed of getting

married. There's a picture of me, aged four, 'marrying' Richard, the vicar's son, on the pavement outside our house, with my two-year-old sister Esther as our brides-maid, and I look very happy about the whole thing; it was my favourite game. In my mind, marriage solved all kinds of problems, like the need to work out what to do with my life and where to do it. I would just hitch myself to some charismatic, confident and decisive chap, and see where we got to. So when Mark told me as he drove me home from our first date that when he proposed to me it would be somewhere memorable, it didn't spook me as it maybe should have done.

Mark was eight years my senior, a physics teacher (and still no alarm bells!), and a passionate Christian with a firm and simple faith based on the kind of certi-tude you find on fridge magnets: 'Smile – God's in control!'; 'Faith is never asking why!' or, 'Ask and you shall receive!' He was certain I was the one, and he took charge in a way that made me feel safe and looked after, but soon became suffocating. I was very frightened about the future, sure, but having my future mapped out by Mark wasn't helping. I started to keep a list of pros and cons in the back of my journal, and the cons side just kept growing.

One night, about six months into the relationship, I had a vivid dream. It was our wedding day, and I was walking down the aisle of a vast, shadowy cathedral in a black wedding dress. Everybody there was quietly weeping, including me. I woke up and knew that if I chose to marry Mark, as he was by that stage fairly persistent in asking me to do, it would feel like the end of my life rather than a happy new beginning.

After we broke up, I decided I needed a two-year detox. The idea landed in my mind with such suddenness and clarity that I've often wondered since if it was God who put it there. Whether divinely inspired or not, I knew I needed to figure out who I was and what kind of a life I wanted for myself, because this tactic of deferring to a strong man was going badly. So I was single for my third year at Birmingham, and then off I went to Canada to study theology and find God and myself. And I would like to stress that I did it because I wanted to, not because my dad suggested it! (Oh, how I hope that's true.)

Fast forward two years from the day of the break-up, I was working on the tills at the college bookstore when a fellow student asked me on a date as I rung up his purchase (*The Wound of Knowledge* by Rowan Williams, in case you were wondering). The student's name was Shawn, I said yes, and the rest, as they say, is history.

I've told you about Shawn's background. It couldn't be more different from mine. We are not remotely similar in terms of temperament, interests or culture, and we can't talk about politics without me crying. So how do I explain that he felt like home, right from the very start? Being with Shawn was the easiest thing in the world. I didn't have to write a single list of pros and cons – I knew I couldn't imagine life without him, and he didn't want to live without me. He wasn't who I would have dreamed up as my perfect life partner; he was better. He has the most amazing brain – an intelligence that challenges and stimulates me on a daily basis. He makes me laugh until I hiccough and fall off my chair. He refuses to prop me up and forces me to stand on my own two feet; he respects me and celebrates me when I do something brave. His commitment to me is absolute.

We got engaged seven months after that first date, in the beautiful Canadian Rockies. We'd driven the thirty hours to Minneapolis so I could meet his family, and we were on our way back to Vancouver. Surrounded by mountains, streams of melting ice, soaring birds and all kinds of wildlife, we read Psalm 104 and thanked God with all our hearts that he had 'satisfied [us] with good things'.

Our wedding was in Oxford, at St Aldate's, where my uncle is rector. Most people, including us, had to travel substantial distances to get there, but the same would have been true of any venue we chose. We had no money, and neither did our families, but one after another, people gave us gifts – from our amazing friends Mo and Ewan who cooked all our guests an extravagant feast, to my bridesmaids who covered the costs of hair and make-up, to our artist friend Tiphanie who painted invites and paid for the printing, to my housemate Kate who bought our wedding rings, to the anonymous person who settled the invoice for the hall where we held the reception. It was an outpouring of generosity that bathed our marriage in blessing from the outset.

We went on honeymoon to Italy – another gift – and then returned to Canada, where we expected to settle. If you've ever been to Vancouver, you'll know why this seemed like a good idea. It is always high up on any chart of the best cities in the world. I moved into the basement Shawn was renting and we began married life.

It wasn't quite the bliss we'd anticipated, but not because of anything to do with our relationship. When we left our wedding in a hire car covered in shaving foam and streamers, we waved goodbye to just under two hundred people who really mattered to us, and I realised I had no idea when we would next see most of them. I found it devastating, and sank fast and deep into depression. Our first months as a married couple were blighted by my dark mood and constant tears. Shawn would come home from lectures to find me under the bedcovers, unable to move or speak. It must have been utterly horrifying for him, but he never let on. I was used to sitting at the bottom of my pit in awful solitude, but here I was with someone who insisted on climbing in there with me. It was humiliating, to say the least. I didn't want anyone knowing how wretched I felt. However painful this period of time, there was one precious gift: the dawning realisation that I had a home with Shawn and he wasn't going to evict me, however horrendous I was to live with. The permanence of the situation became crystal clear: if he could love me in this state, he wasn't going anywhere.

Finding you are locked into a shared life with someone can be both reassuringly secure and terrifyingly claustrophobic. For me it felt something like taking out a massive thirty-five-year mortgage on a property you absolutely love – it's still scary to know you will never, ever be able to sell it, however you may feel about it in the future. In those early days I developed an image in my head: that marriage was a bit like having a cat strapped to my chest. It could be snuggly and sweet, purring away and keeping me company, or it could get feisty and scratch me and its fur could make me feel itchy and uncomfortably warm. Either way, the cat was there. No getting away from it.

Thinking about marriage as a lifelong deal is becoming less common. In our society it is relatively easy to unstrap the cat, so to speak. Divorces can be granted on a 'no-fault' basis, simply because one or both parties no longer wish to be bound by their commitment. If we allow ourselves a get-out clause, or if we so much as suspect our spouse has an exit strategy, the foundations of the marriage become dangerously weak. Feeling locked in to marriage might be uncomfortable, frightening even, but it also gives you no choice but to make the most of the situation.

So Shawn and I were settling in to life together in Vancouver; I was trying to climb out of my depression; and we were making plans to start the process of applying to become Canadian citizens when – in the middle of a long night, about six months in – I came to a sudden realisation: no one had *made* me live so far away from all these people I loved. I hadn't been exiled, like Napoleon. I got up, found a pen and paper, and did what I so often do when a momentous decision needs to be made: I wrote two lists – reasons to stay in Vancouver, and reasons to move to England. The reasons for moving to England were weighty and numerous, and by morning I knew I had to start what I assumed would be a long and hard conversation with Shawn. I would be asking him to give up the life he'd imagined, in a culture he understood and knew how to navigate, to go to a country that I'd really not done a good job of promoting, since until that night I'd had no intention of ever living there again.

I broached the subject in the car the next day – a good place to have the kind of discussion that might lead to a desire to run away before everything has been said. As I reached the end of my speech, we were crossing the Port Mann Bridge outside Vancouver in heavy rain. I think I wound up by saying something like, 'So really what I'm trying to explain is I think I'd like us to go and live in England.' There was a pause – a very short one, all things considered. And then Shawn said, 'OK. Let's do it.' Of all the times and in all the ways Shawn has shown me love over our years together, that short sentence stands in sharp relief. He made a sacrificial, life-altering decision in a matter of seconds, simply because he understood how much it mattered to me.

I had finished my studies, but Shawn had a year to go. During that year we made our preparations for the big move – job-hunting, whittling down our possessions, and sorting paperwork. I'd done lots of moving and I knew how it worked, but this felt different. Shawn and I would be getting on the plane together, and we would be together on the other side, unpacking and settling in to a new place. This time, when I moved, not everything would be different.

As I sit here writing, Shawn is working in the room

next door – in other words, within shouting distance. 'Shawn?' I call out, too lazy to get up and walk the eight paces to his side. He doesn't answer but I know he can hear me, so I keep going. 'How long will we have been married on our next wedding anniversary?' 'What? You don't know?' 'No.' 'Don't worry, I don't know either.' Fortunately he's better at numbers than I am, so he can work it out. 'If we got married in 2003, it will be fourteen years.' We did, so he must be right.

That's a good long time. I'm proud of us! We've lived in four houses, had two children and one cat, paid off our student debt and worked hard in challenging jobs. We decided before we got married that we would never use the word 'divorce' in our relationship – in seriousness or in jest. I think it was a good decision. We've had horrendous fights, gone through periods where life got too busy and we lost touch with each other, faced significant issues that raise their ugly heads with monotonous frequency and which we have yet to decapitate. I have come to accept that Shawn is someone who goes shopping for fun (a concept I can't get my head around at all), drinks Coke and doesn't enjoy picnics, and he has come to accept that I will never be excited by the annual Apple technology launch and am constantly filling our house with people he barely knows. We also know each other better than anyone else does and, in spite of that, we are each quietly confident that the person we married is the best human being ever to walk the planet. We still get so engrossed in conversation that we miss our turn-off on the motorway on a regular basis. We are homesick for each other when we're apart, and there is nothing more restful than being alone together.

A bed of thorny roses

The truth of life is that it often plays out in a messy, painful way, even for those who, like David, declare their desire to please God with every fibre of their being. We are wounded and we wound. We are driven by lust, greed and fear. We catch glimpses of the wholeness and beauty of God's design for marriage, and yet we make choices that deny us the joy he intended for us. Even in loving, lifelong, adultery-free marriages, alienating, harmful words and actions are inevitable because we are human, and we may be redeemed but we are not yet fully transformed. This is why home must be more than marriage. If we expect our need for belonging, stability, safety, comfort, continuity, acceptance – all those things that together make a person feel at home – to be met in just one relationship, we will make ourselves more vulnerable to homelessness than anyone ought to be.

A Severe Mercy, by Sheldon Vanauken,[9] is the story of an attempt to create a relationship so intimate, intense and all-consuming that it destroys the boundaries between the two individuals and heals the loneliness that exists in the core of all other humans. Davy and Van set about putting their love above all else, making a vow they called 'the shining barrier' – a vow to share everything: work, friendship, interests. They even decided not to have children because they could not experience parenthood in the same way. If any marriage could be considered an unassailable fortress, it would be this one. But Van would later come to call their relationship 'a pagan marriage, invaded by Christ'. Davy became a Christian while the couple lived in Oxford, partly due to a friendship with C. S. Lewis, and Van reluctantly followed, as the shining barrier required him to. They returned to America and continued to explore faith together until Davy contracted a virus that ultimately killed her at only forty years old. Remarkably, it was through the loss of her that Van finally found his own way to God's heart. His love of Davy, as he came to see, was idolatry, and while he worshipped at another altar he would never be able to give Christ undivided devotion. He wrote, 'That death, so full of suffering for us both, suffering that still overwhelmed my life, was yet a severe mercy. A mercy as severe as death, a severity as merciful as love.'

Marriage is a gift of God, and a good marriage is a source of strength, love and hope, not only for the two at the centre but for everyone else in its orbit. But marriage was never designed to meet the deepest of human needs. Mike Mason, in his beautiful meditation *The Mystery of Marriage,* writes, 'It is an enormous source of human frustration that our need for intimacy far outstrips its capacity to be met in other people.' We want to believe the Disney myth that a wedding is both the happy ending and the beginning of a perfectly contented and fulfilled life. But the slightest brush with reality shatters what is after all just an entertaining illusion. That conclusion might seem incredibly bleak, but the frustration itself points us to a greater truth, if we will listen to it and not just struggle against it. Mason continues, 'In each one of us the holiest and neediest and most sensitive place of all has been made and is reserved for God alone, so that only He can enter there.'[10]

CHAPTER EIGHT

Right here

My neighbourhood is my home

Vancouver, Canada

*'Dear old world', she murmured, 'you are very lovely,
and I am glad to be alive in you.'*

L. M. Montgomery, *Anne of Green Gables*

FINDING A JOB from halfway round the world had its challenges, but as often happens in this life, knowing the right people can help. My parents were thrilled we were headed back their way and immediately sent news of Shawn's availability out on the bush telegraph.

We went over to England for the Christmas before the summer we planned to relocate and spent a day at a church with an upcoming youth pastor vacancy. It wasn't quite

145

what we'd thought we were after; Shawn wasn't convinced about the idea of working for the Church of England and we had pictured ourselves in a northern city, not an affluent village in the south. But by the time we'd met all the church staff, toured the environs, asked and answered dozens of penetrating questions, everyone involved had a sense that this appointment was going to happen.

Having made the snap decision to make a life in England, we'd talked endlessly about what we wanted for our future and the values we wanted to shape how our story played out from here. Both of us had moved many times and until this point had seen our location as an incidental coordinate on a map. This next move was our chance to experiment with commitment. We wanted to start our lives in the next place with the assumption that we would stay for the indefinite future; there would be no escape plan lined up. This was both exhilarating and frightening, perhaps in the same way the idea of moving might be to someone who has always lived in one place.

The following June we said painful but resolute good-byes to Vancouver before spending two months in France with my parents, during which Shawn finished his last essays while I ate vast quantities of French bread and swam in the village swimming pool. Then it was time to see what settling down would be like. Shawn's new job came with accommodation, a three-storey town house with no garden, but only a stone's throw from the village green. Chalfont St Peter is a proper village, with a high street where you quickly get to know enough people to see familiar faces every few yards. We intended to love it and, thankfully, it was the kind of place that made it easy.

It was stressful having to figure out the details of daily life from scratch – where to buy food, how rubbish collection worked, who had priority at a crossroads, not to mention who to call if you needed either company (me), or the right kind of wire to hook one bit of technology to another (Shawn) – but it helped that once we'd figured it out we wouldn't have to go through the process again for a long time – perhaps ever.

Part of me thinks now how ridiculous I was to assume I could just decide to settle down come what may. I'd swung the pendulum, clung on and ridden it merrily to the extreme end of its parabola. But there's a begrudging admiration for my old self there too. This might have been an experiment, but I was giving it my all. I was determined to force roots into this particular ground. I'm sure this attitude helped me through the early days when nothing felt right and my surroundings struck me as appallingly unexciting and domesticated. I held on to a word of advice given to us as we went through security at Vancouver Airport for the last time: 'It always takes at least two years to feel at home somewhere'. I tried not to panic as wave after wave of homesickness hit: homesickness for Canada, for Portugal, for France, for anywhere-but-here.

Reflecting back on those thoughts, feelings and plans, I think I'd stumbled on a kernel of truth, albeit packaged in a misapprehension. The truth was that arriving in this new place with the intention of bedding in so totally was exactly what I needed to do; I'd go as far as to say, I think it's exactly how everyone should approach new places. The theologian Walter Brueggemann writes, 'Our humanness cannot be found in escape, detachment, absence of commitment, and undefined freedom . . . a yearning for a place is a decision to enter history with an identifiable people in an identifiable pilgrimage.'[1] The misapprehension was that in order to invest in a place I would need to be pretty sure I wasn't going to leave it any time soon. Which of us can make reliable plans for next week, let alone for a couple of decades hence? All we can do is to live the best we can in the present moment, holding the future on an open palm. When you part company with a Portuguese friend, they'll often say, 'See you later, *se Deus quiser*' – if God wills it. Depending on how you take it, there could be some fatalism to it, but it's a healthy reminder of reality at the same time. The understanding I've come to now is that however temporary our stay, we need to give *this place* our full attention, loyalty and love.

I recently discovered an online magazine for Third Culture Kids, Denizenmag.com. An article by Mareike Pietzsch expresses beautifully the challenges of a decision to stay somewhere instead of moving on. Mareike was born in Namibia and has lived in South Africa, South Korea, Ireland and Germany. In 2013, having lived in the German city of Hamburg for a very respectable three years, the end of a work contract opened up a world of possibilities. Spoilt for choice, she turned to her mother for advice. Her mother told her to stay where she was. It wasn't what she wanted to hear – for her, moving was the easier option – but she decided to accept the challenge. What she found as she dug in for a longer stay was that she was faced with layers of reality that a tourist to Hamburg can skim over; she had to 'embrace its dents, smudges and cultural nuances'. But she also reaped the benefits of relationships given time to mature, finding she had friends who would bring over chicken soup if she was sick and organise surprise birthday parties for her. Writing about the experience, she says:

My taste for adventure has not simply vanished. I still get 'itchy feet' when I want to pack up and leave. When routine stifles me, I follow every whim. If I feel like visiting another city, I do. If I feel like wandering through the city of Hamburg, exploring nooks and crannies, I do. Spontaneity is my best friend. And my need for freedom is sated through exploration – my eyes or my camera, my only companion – as I wander along the harbour or past Altbau buildings as the sun sets and the wind whispers its secrets . . .

Staying put, so to speak, has been both a decision and a gradual process. Recently, I bought myself a beautiful wrought iron bed. This purchase marked the beginning of my choice to stay in Hamburg. It marked the beginning of letting down my anchor in this here – my here.[2]

Know your place

I found Mareike on Twitter and we corresponded for a while. It was no surprise to discover she's living in

South Africa now, but I know she made Hamburg her home while she was there. She explored and observed and got to know it. It is entirely possible in this day and age to live somewhere that never becomes 'your place'. Our neighbours are a couple in their late forties. They leave early each morning for jobs in far corners of the city, they travel extensively and they are working towards an early retirement they plan to split between Thailand and Portugal. They picked out this area as a place to live because it is equidistant to their respective workplaces, has a buoyant property market and a low crime rate. Their relationship to Surbiton is superficial, no different from many millions of others whose address is nothing more than the location of their stuff and their letterbox. And does it really matter? What really is the significance of place? Christopher Tilley expresses it thus: 'Places form landscapes and landscape may be defined as sets of relational places each embodying (literally and metaphorically) emotions, memories, and associations derived from personal and interpersonal shared experience.'[3]

Does it matter if we live without regard for place? Yes. It really does.

Craig Bartholomew believes that 'We live amidst a crisis of place'; that place has become 'something that one moves through, preferably at great speed'. In a very literal sense, I moved through Chalfont St Peter very slowly. I'd passed my driving test five years earlier but had never had a car to drive, and as a result I'd become slightly phobic about the entire concept. We were very

kindly given an elderly VW Polo by a church member's
son who, impressively, was giving up life behind the
wheel for ethical reasons, but the truth is I was much
happier walking or cycling. This gave me the chance to
discover a shortcut across the common where a thicket
of wild raspberries grew. I stumbled on a secretive
police dog training centre and a stretch of woodland
scattered with creepy burnt-out cars. I worked out the
gradient of the land well enough to avoid the steepest
hills, and which stretches of road were most liable to
flooding. I saw a beautiful but neglected old house
demolished and replaced with four cookie-cutter
new-builds and I read signs on lampposts alerting
passers-by to lost cats and keys. When I dropped my
own keys one winter, shortly before a heavy snowfall,
it was only because I was on foot two weeks later that
I saw the notice pinned to a fence letting me know
they'd been found. I had frequent surreal conversations
with a middle-aged lady who wore pink knee socks and
a green woollen dress, and who struggled with what I
assumed must be paranoid schizophrenia; she was
convinced I was following her, although our paths
mostly crossed as we headed in opposite directions. I
knew by face if not by name the elderly gentleman who
passed his days on the bench outside the fish and chip
shop, and the teens who congregated outside our local
corner shop. Raj, who ran the shop and lived next door,
let us have milk and pay for it the next time, and didn't
bat an eyelid when Shawn occasionally popped in for
something early in the morning in his dressing gown

and slippers. I became friends with the manager of the bookshop on the high street; she would make me tea and I'd sit on the step-stool meant for reaching high shelves and chat with her in between customers. Over the years I watched three local children with open fascination as they grew up seemingly in some kind of time-warp; dressed in clothes from the 1930s, hair in long braids in the case of the girls, the boy's side parting slicked down with Brylcreem, they rambled the countryside with butterfly nets and jam jars full of newts and tadpoles. I never managed to get to the bottom of what was going on there.

There are many things to know about a place, and I only scratched the surface. Every 'here' has a history, a geology, a biology, and a mysterious and complex web of connections that bind it to its inhabitants and the wider world. I've never been able to muster much enthusiasm about birds, so all I ever really paid attention to were the flashy red kites that soar dramatically over the Chiltern Hills once more. Bluebells carpeted the woodlands a short walk from our house every spring, but there aren't many more wildflowers I could identify by name. I've no idea what the local soil type was, and although a sign proudly claimed Chalfont St Peter as a 'Domesday book' village, I never boned up on local history. So when I say, in a slightly reproving manner, that our lack of curiosity for the places in which we live is remiss, I am lecturing myself as well as you. Why remiss, you ask? Well, because God intends us to make the place we live home, to tend it and enable it to thrive. And as Regent College professors Loren and Mary Ruth Wilkinson write, 'We are more careful of the little and large bits of creation placed directly (and indirectly) into our care when we know them well.'[4]

Where we live is not incidental. What can you see from your front door? Who lives on your street? Where are the green spaces and who uses them? Who is hurting and why, and what can be done to reach out and help? When and where does the community gather – are there street parties or police forums, festivals, parades or protests? Who are the leaders in the area, and who holds them to account? What is the racial and religious make-up of the area, and what can be done to further peace and cohesion? Love is more than a feeling: it is a choice to commit to and seek the good of the other. We may live in a vast city, a sprawling suburb or a rural hamlet, but wherever we live, to properly love our neighbourhood is a true challenge, and the first step is to get to know it.

The second step is to look after it. We sometimes use the word 'stewardship' when talking about our role in God's world, a word that originates in an Old English word for 'sty-warden' or pig keeper. (Incidentally, while we are on the porcine theme, my married name derives from swine herder too. Suddenly, pigs are everywhere you look!) 'Stewardship' is the word used to translate the Greek word *oikonomia* – not oinkonomia, which would be pretty funny – and *oikos* means household. Woven into the meaning of stewardship, therefore, is the concept of the earth as our home. We are to look after God's world because it's his; he loves it and so it is honouring to him for us to take good care of it – but also because if we turn it into a pigsty, we have to live in a pigsty. The consequences of poor stewardship are already felt, mostly by those around the world who can't afford to install air-conditioning, pump in clean water, and import the best of harvests from elsewhere when their own are devastated by floods, droughts, pests or erosion. Each of us is responsible for how we live in our patch, but each patch is part of one quilt, and the quilt needs to keep us all warm.

Loving the unlovable place

Some places are – on the face of it – easier to love. They are the kind of places that cause holidaymakers to spend fevered hours on property websites, dreaming of what it would be like to have longer than an annual fortnight to feast on the views. And then there are places passed over by those with any degree of choice about where to live. Shadwell is one such place, and yet it is where my youngest sister Beth has made her home for the last eight years. Situated in East London, it is an area facing consid-erable challenges. It boasts the highest rate of child poverty in the country, a fifth of its residents are long-term unemployed, and its housing is overcrowded, appallingly expensive and substandard. When Beth and her husband Matt moved into their flat, the walls were furred with mould, and within weeks they had a bedbug infestation. The Docklands Light Railway runs past just metres from their bedroom, and for months they got no sleep as blazing lights and heavy machinery operated between midnight and 5 a.m., upgrading the line for wealthy commuters living the dream in their high-rise Docklands apartments. Their entire block was covered in blue netting while windows were replaced, and the flat above them seemed to be undergoing perpetual renovation, involving the noisiest of power tools.

You might think they moved here because they'd exhausted all options, but no. This was their number one option, and by and large they've been really happy there. Beth has had Bengali lessons so she can better connect with her neighbours; she's taught English as a second language, volunteered for the local food-bank, started a community garden called 'the Shadpatch', and relaunched a toddler group that had closed down. She's worked part-time as a nurse and become a mother, and I've seen her thrive in what to me seems a hugely challenging environment. Reflecting on what has changed both in her and in their community while living there she said, 'I think we feel a lot more contented with materialistic simplicity and with deepening friendships and community now. We are still learning about how to be vulnerable and authentic but trust that will be a lifelong process.

'I think we've become a little less idealistic about what it looks like to change the world, but with higher expectations of God and his power and grace. It's always really easy to believe you can change things just by wanting it enough or trying harder. Sometimes things don't make sense, some things work and some things don't for reasons you don't understand. Good friends of ours told us early on that God was here before we moved in and would be here after we left and just to be grateful to be part of what he's already doing.'

Many of the challenges associated with living in a neighbourhood such as Shadwell can be attributed to the built environment itself. Architecture has enormous influence on the way a community functions, whether it fosters division or cohesion, whether it encourages interaction or causes isolation. In May 2016, an architect, trapped in the beleaguered city of Homs in Syria, recorded a TED talk.[5] Marwa Al-Sabouni has lived through six years of war. Half of the city, including her home and her offices, is now rubble. In her view, architecture has played a crucial role in creating, amplifying and sustaining the conflict. Urban planners, under the guise of making 'improvements', zoned the community by class, economics and religion, with disastrous consequences. Marwa says, speaking with almost inconceivable courage and optimism:

Hopefully the war will end, and the question that as an architect I have to ask is: how do we rebuild? What are the principles that we should adopt in order to avoid repeating the same mistakes? . . . Our built environment matters. The fabric of our cities is reflected in the fabric of our souls. And whether in the shape of informal concrete slums or broken social housing or trampled old towns or forests of skyscrapers, the contemporary urban archetypes that have emerged all across the Middle East have been one cause of the alienation and fragmentation of our communities.

We can learn from this. We can learn how to rebuild in another way, how to create an architecture that doesn't contribute only to the practical and economic aspects of people's lives, but also to their social, spiritual and psychological needs. Those needs were totally overlooked in the Syrian cities before the war. We need to create again cities that are shared by the communities that inhabit them. If we do so, people will not feel the need to seek identities opposed to the other identities all around, because they will all feel at home.

Perhaps you live somewhere where the buildings conspire to make you feel you don't belong. There are certainly neighbourhoods that it takes more work to love. But the challenge for all of us is to accept the reality of our context in the present moment, and to do what we can to serve and improve it.

Zion

David had lived in Hebron as king of Judah for seven and a half years when he was made king of Israel too, uniting the tribes into one nation. Hebron was in the south, and he needed a capital somewhere that made sense in the new circumstances. Jerusalem was perfectly situated on the spine running through the centre of the land but had never been captured by either Israel or Judah. For centuries the Jebusites had lived unassailed in this small, walled fortress-city, even as battles raged around them between Hebrews, Philistines and Amalekites. Received wisdom has it that the city was impregnable but seeing as, once David chose it for his seat of government, all he had to do was climb through the water shaft with a few other men to capture it, I have to assume there was a good reason no one captured it. Perhaps it was a bit bleak and uninviting, or the houses were squat and the streets poorly laid out. Maybe it had bad drainage and an unpleasant odour. Whatever the attractions of the city, or lack thereof, Jerusalem was now David's place. He took up residence and immediately began to make improvements; 'he built up the area around it, from the terraces inward' (2 Samuel 5:9). Psalm 122 gives us a sense of the significance Jerusalem came to have to David personally but also to the whole people of Israel:

Our feet are standing
in your gates, Jerusalem.

Jerusalem is built like a city
that is closely compacted together.
That is where the tribes go up –
the tribes of the LORD *–*
to praise the name of the LORD

according to the statute given to Israel.
There stand the thrones for judgment,
the thrones of the house of David.

Pray for the peace of Jerusalem:
'May those who love you be secure.
May there be peace within your walls
and security within your citadels.'
For the sake of my family and friends,
I will say, 'Peace be within you.'
For the sake of the house of the LORD *our God,*
I will seek your prosperity.[6]

David's choice of Jerusalem as his capital city turned it into somewhere that, in Eugene Peterson's words, 'formed the nucleus for a rich gathering of images, symbols, promises and visions that express God's sovereign purposes worked out on the hard, inhospitable ground of our lives'.[7] Jerusalem, meaning 'City of Peace', was where Jesus paid for the ultimate peace treaty with his life, dying on the outskirts, buried in its rock, resurrected to walk again on its soil. As he approached its walls for the last time, Luke records that he wept over it. Even with the ordeal he knew faced him, his grief was for the future of the city and its people: 'The days will come upon you when your enemies will build an embankment against you and encircle you and hem you in on every side. They will dash you to the ground, you and the children within your walls. They will not leave one stone on another.'[8] In AD 70, just a few decades later, Jerusalem was utterly destroyed following a siege by the Romans under the emperor Titus.

One of the justifications given for ill-treating or neglecting the welfare of the planet is the belief that it has no eternal future. It isn't surprising that atheists should hold this belief, but it's both sad and a bit shocking that the idea that God plans to eliminate the whole physical universe at the end of time still persists in some Christian circles. My friend's little girl told her at bedtime the other night that she didn't want to go to heaven because she liked her body and didn't want to be a wispy ghost. My friend didn't know how to reassure her. She'd been taught that 'spiritual' means non-physical, so she also thought heaven would probably be light and air and sound and not much else. We had a very exciting conversation about the biblical picture of the redemption of the whole creation.[9]

Jerusalem had its heyday in David's time, or possibly his son Solomon's. In its five-thousand-year history, it has been besieged twenty-three times, attacked fifty-two times, captured and recaptured forty-four times and utterly destroyed twice. (Thank you, Wikipedia, for this neat summary.) Following the Arab–Israeli war in 1948, the city was divided. The western half became part of the new political state of Israel, and the east, including the Old City, was annexed by Jordan. During the Six Day War in 1967, the Israel Defence Forces captured the eastern part, evicted its residents and demolished hundreds of homes. This, then, is no city of peace. During the first decade and a half of the twenty-first century, the entire region has remained in acute danger of descending into chaos as religions and ideologies have clashed, battles have been fought over land, water and oil, and ancient grudges continue to drive wedges between ethnic groups living side by side. There have been 149 bombings in Jerusalem since the year 2000.

But I don't think for a minute that God has given up on it: a new Jerusalem is the crowning glory of John's vision of a restored and redeemed earth in the book of Revelation, constructed from precious metals, pearls and jewels. The new Jerusalem is built on the foundations of the past. The language is strange to our ears, and clearly not to be understood literally, but here are the twelve tribes of Israel, the kings and the nations that have spent all of history intent on mutual destruction, living together within the city walls, worshipping the same God. It is a city full of light. Its inhabitants are healthy, happy and fearless. We can live in hope that one day we will live in this city, and we'll never have to leave.

In the meantime, we live here, and perhaps here is hard. But consider this – Marwa Al-Sabouni's city of Homs is not the city she grew up in: the economy is at a standstill; most of the major landmarks have been razed to the ground; many of her friends have fled or been killed. And yet she remains committed to its future. It is still her place. It is still her home. If Marwa can call Homs home, we can call our neighbourhood, wherever it may be and whatever its challenges, home.

CHAPTER NINE

Bricks and mortar

My house is my home

It was a mistake to think of houses, old houses, as being empty. They were filled with memories, with the faded echoes of voices. Drops of tears, drops of blood, the ring of laughter, the edge of tempers that had ebbed and flowed between the walls, into the walls, over the years.

Nora Roberts, *Key of Knowledge*

SHAWN AND I have taken to going to occasional comedy evenings, the kind of thing hosted in dark, sticky rooms in the back of local pubs. You pay £5 to listen to a mixed bag of stand-ups, some of whom are famous and most of

163

whom are funny. One time, the comedian Russell Howard was there. He had a great riff going about the poverty he'd endured once taking up comedy as a full-time profession. Looking for somewhere to live, he had asked the estate agent why all the property details he'd been shown were basements. 'That's all there is in your budget I'm afraid,' came the answer. 'Great,' he said. 'I am now too poor to live above the surface of the earth.' He moved into one of these basements, and his father came over for a visit. His father was positive and encouraging while he was shown around, until his son announced his plan to get a dog. 'Oh no,' his dad said flatly. 'You couldn't let a dog live down here.'

Having been a basement-dweller myself in Vancouver, when I first saw the house in Chalfont St Peter, my joy that I would be living above ground overrode all else. There is something to be said for setting the accommodation bar very low and upgrading with every move, as I have done through my married life to this point. It makes you grateful for things you might have been at risk of taking for granted, like daylight, and a ceiling high enough to allow you to stand up straight.

We lived at our first house in Chalfont St Peter for six years in total, and if I were showing you around now (without a sales agenda), this is what you'd see: when you walk in the front door, there's a toilet on your left, a utility room straight ahead and a room off to the side which used to be a garage and still feels as though it would be more suited to keeping a car than being used for any other purpose. (We used it as storage for youth equipment during the church building project, for youth groups and leader meetings once said project was completed, and as sleeping quarters for the various people who lived with us during our tenure.) Now go up the first set of very steep stairs (down which I was known to fall now and then – funny to watch, less funny to experience), and you have a bathroom, then a multi-tasker of a room that served as our dining room, sitting room, study and guest bedroom, with a hole in the wall leading through to a little kitchen. Up another set of stairs are two reasonably sized bedrooms and a box room.

The previous occupants had painted the walls of the stairwell in two colours from top to bottom of the house, with the lower half a deep maroon, which as you may remember was the colour of my school uniform and there-fore clearly had to go. Other than their addition of maroon and our attempt to expunge it, the house was not decorated in any way for fifteen years. When I took baths I would shut my eyes, not because I was relaxing into the experi-ence but because I didn't want to look at the cracked, mottled black and green plasterwork sagging ominously over my head. The cupboards in the kitchen were too shallow for anything other than mugs and single rows of tins, so what counter space we had was entirely taken up with piles of plates, cereal boxes and dying basil plants. The walls were paper thin, so we unwillingly eaves-dropped on the domestic dramas of our Sri Lankan neighbours. Behind the house was an alleyway where dodgy deals were made behind the bins, and foxes mated with noisy, violent passion.

We left Vancouver with our most treasured possessions – artwork, books and photo albums – but nothing practical, because we were limited by our airline luggage allowance. I'm a firm believer that a lot of what makes a house a home is familiar objects: the misshapen pottery milk jug made for you by your sister, the decorative plate with your children's footprints on, the candlestick that used to be part of a set of two but which fortunately looks fine by itself. My friend Juliette is a foster carer, and she's found personal objects are a huge part of helping children settle in: 'It's been a challenge to work out how to make our house a home for our foster children when they move in, however temporary that might be. Ensuring that their identity is reflected somewhere in the house seems to help – whether that's wall art in their bedroom, family photos on the fridge or a hook for their own towel in the bathroom.'

Everything else we needed and more – bedding, sofas, crockery, a kettle and a fridge, occasional tables galore – was soon provided by kind benefactors, and we were mostly very grateful. But I'm ashamed to confess that I privately hated the chintzy armchairs, I despised the wood-veneer bookshelf with one randomly placed glass shelf, I felt ashamed of the over-plump tasselled cushions. The nineteenth-century textile designer William Morris issued a well-known maxim: 'Have nothing in your house that you do not know to be useful, or believe to be beautiful.' My house would have made him turn in his grave, but what could I do? We'd blown our budget on the maroon cover-up and we had to take what was on offer and make do.

My friend Sophie is married to the rector of a church in the West Midlands, and they have three little ones. She has a strong artistic sensibility and a real flair for interior design, but money has been tight for the past few years. Most of the time she's able to keep a lid on her frustration about certain aspects of her life, but now and then something will trigger a meltdown. 'We went to see my brother-in-law and his family in the house they have just bought recently,' she told me. 'I walked through the door and initially delighted in it with them. Jo, it's gorgeous. But then I started crying. It was so embarrassing, I needed to leave and get some air. They had exactly the furniture they wanted; they hadn't had to accept half-broken things like we had because we'd never be able to afford anything better. The walls were all painted in shades they liked and the curtains and cushions had this amazing mismatched matchiness. Their curtains fitted their windows rather than being extra-long and extra-wide because who-knows-where-they'll-live-next. I was so envious that they had a home that they'd bought, that was theirs to grow up and old in, to make memories in and make an extension of their personalities.'

It isn't just vicars who live in accommodation tied to their work, and who don't have the funds to make the changes they'd like. If you are in the armed forces, the hospitality industry, the health care system, or perhaps working in a boarding school, you may well resonate with Sophie's experience. I know I do.

Our first Chalfont St Peter house wasn't perfect, but it very definitely was home, and became all the more so when first Alexa and then Charis came to live there with us. Alexa was born in early 2007, and Charis in the latter part of 2009, and while neither of them remembers living there, it was their first home, and will always be significant in our family history.

The church had bought the house for whoever came to be their youth pastor, typecasting this person as a young and probably single person. When we became a family of four, however, it was decided – rather amazingly – to upgrade us to a bigger house, again in Chalfont St Peter, but this time with a garden. When I first saw it actual squeals came out of my mouth. I ran around it like an over-excited piglet, hardly daring to believe we were actually going to be allowed to live there. It was a revelation to discover building materials could elicit a deep emotional response: granite worktops, wooden floors, slate tiles; all these reduced me to a state of incoherent joy. Add to the picture a pristine en suite complete with power shower, vast built-in wardrobes and a garden with a patio for barbecues and a shed for junk overflow and this was definitely 'home sweet home'. For three years; at least.

During those nine years as a youth pastor, Shawn had been busy getting ordained on the side and, when he was ready for a new challenge, a house move was always going to be part of the deal. There are huge advantages to working for the Church of England, free housing being one of them. But the housing is also one of the disadvantages, because you never get to choose where you live or experience what it would be like to call your house your own. My friend Anne, another fellow vicar's wife, says she gets a crazy, excited over-the-top feeling of being home when they go camping, because they own their tent. There is clearly something significant about ownership for some people.

This lack of choice combines weirdly with the fact that you would never in a million years be able to afford to buy the house you haven't chosen, and then there may be the expectation that you will host endless church events on the premises, all of which can make it hard to feel at home in church housing. But I have to say that I've found each of the three church houses I've lived in has very much felt like home. And I'm happy to report that house number three has been yet another upgrade.

What makes a house a home?

Of all the ways we might understand home, our physical accommodation carries the greatest burden of expectation. The door we can open with our own keys, the pictures we have chosen to put on the walls, the bed where we lie down and feel secure enough to lose consciousness for hours at a time, the space into which we have the right to invite others: where we live is central to most people's definition of home.

In his fascinating overview of the history of private life, *At Home*, Bill Bryson writes about the fact that although houses can be vastly different, there is something intrinsically resonant of home about them. 'Houses are really quite odd things. They have almost no universally defining qualities: they can be of practically any shape, incorporate virtually any material, be of almost any size. Yet wherever we go in the world we know houses and recognise domesticity the moment we see them. This aura of homeliness is, it turns out, extremely ancient.'[1]

The significance of houses as homes is heavily influenced by culture and history. The English place a huge value on property ownership. Seventy-five per cent of UK residents owned property at the start of the twenty-first century, in comparison to half or fewer of the Swiss, the Germans and the Austrians. The goal of buying one's own home is shared by the majority of adults in the United Kingdom, and whether or not this is attainable for the masses is an oft-discussed subject in the press, the pub and the halls of Westminster. There is an unspoken consensus that if you've got a mortgage on the place where you live, it will feel like your home in a way rented accommodation never could. I have always hoped that wouldn't be the case, because I'm resigned to living in church housing until my dotage, but as I've been listening to stories about home over the last few months, it does seem to be a bit of a theme. Take Paula, who wrote to me saying, 'When I was renting after my marriage broke up, I didn't feel I could make it our home due to all the permissions we had to have just to knock a nail in the wall. Now I have a mortgage I am free to make a home.' Reading that made my anxiety levels shoot up, and I tried to get her to qualify what she was saying: 'That's one of the things I've been thinking about – the connection between owning and feeling at home. I've never lived somewhere I or my family owned, so I don't know what the difference is. I would imagine the divorce would have unsettled you even if you had moved into somewhere you owned straightaway, but I could be wrong?'

Paula wasn't able to give me the reassurance I was fishing for. 'Yes, it did at first, but once I was ready to truly move on emotionally, by making a place ours, the knowledge I had to get permission to even decorate was prohibitive to healing. I had previously lived in a church rental and we could do what we wanted, but it still didn't feel the same. There's something about ownership, not just of the bricks and mortar but of the space . . .'

I might never live in a property I own, but I can still put my stamp on my home. One of our favourite national pastimes is home improvement. The United Kingdom is peppered with vast superstores selling paint, coving, wallpaper, and equipment for removing said wallpaper the following year, and more showerhead designs than you could have imagined possible. Magazines and television shows keep us all up to date on interior design trends lest we should be tempted to stop tinkering (a disaster for the DIY industry), and we are encouraged to make sure our home environment reflects our personality and sense of style in much the same way as the fashion industry tells us our clothing ought to. For those who need a helping hand to keep them current, there are plenty of sages around to tell us what is what. According to Ali Morris in her article on the website interiordesign.net, 'As modern life gets busier and more pressured, our homes have become our sanctuaries. Centered around simplicity, serenity and seamlessness, the 2016 interior reflects our need to switch off and detox. Warm but calming colors are complemented by natural textures and soft shapes while furniture is becoming ever more tailored and intuitive.'[2] In 2015 we were being urged to use strong colours and add bold, luxurious touches inspired by the world of glitz and glamour. It all seems terribly trivial and consumerist and makes me want to go undercover and lay swirly carpet in upmarket residences under cover of night. (Picture me in balaclava and black tracksuit bottoms cackling with maniacal glee as I unroll colourful chaos over acres of peaceful neutrality.) However, I have to concede it is easier to feel at home in surroundings we find aesthetically pleasing. My friend Rachel recently got married to a lovely man and moved into the house he runs as a bed and breakfast. For her, making it home has been a matter of sorting out clashing colours, trying to get their respective possessions to 'work together' – and persuading him to relinquish some of his many doorstops, thriftily made by filling plastic bottles with water. We feel at home when our surroundings reflect our aesthetics – to a degree at least.

Some houses have every reason to feel like home and yet don't, and others feel like home immediately even if there's no rational explanation for it. When my Russian friend Julia was a child, her family rented a small white country house – a *dacha*, traditionally the summer homes of city-dwellers. She says, 'It was home from the first sight, even before there were personal things in it. The only understanding or explanation I've got is that the house was a perfect real representation of my inner home, my psychic structure. Somehow it was "my size".'

If we are going to be truly at home where we live, we can't leave our hearts elsewhere. We can't expect to make our houses homes if we are really still thinking of home as the last place we lived, or the place before that. For people who grew up in one house, a house full of happy memories and significant personal history, it can be particularly challenging to relocate the feeling of home to a new address, especially if there are parents still living in that childhood home long after you became an adult. I've heard lots of my grown-up friends talk about 'going home' when they are off to see their mum and dad and will be sleeping in their childhood bedroom. It makes sense on one level, but if they really do think of it that way, it must make where they live now less of a home.

My friend Fi's story perfectly illustrates how problematic this attachment can be. She says, 'I grew up in the same house and didn't move out until I got married, so that house felt well and truly like home. We had a massive kitchen table and Mum would feed anybody and everybody who came through.' Tragically, Fi's mum developed cancer and died when Fi was in her mid-teens.

I got married and moved three years after Mum died and, shortly after, Dad remarried. There was a lot of heartache at how things were changing in our family home. I had a new husband and a new house, but that was still my home! I couldn't bear things being changed or moved about and I became wildly possessive.

I remember a physical sense of relief the day they sold the house and moved on. I expected to feel devastated but it allowed me to let go of the sadness wrapped up in that place. It had always felt incomplete without Mum. Suddenly I felt able to leave the past and fully immerse myself in making my new home with Trevor, filling it with our own memories. My dad and his new wife's house is a lovely neutral place for everyone to gather, but my home is now my proper home.

So what makes a house a home?

We will all answer that question differently, but we'll probably mention some or all of the following: ownership, the people who live there with us, the physical contents and the ability to personalise the décor, the memories that have been made there, the setting and the neighbours. My mum has moved numerous times throughout her life, and has given the idea of home a lot of thought:

When it comes to houses, beauty and hospitality are more important to me than size. Small can be beautiful and meals can be simple and people can sleep almost anywhere. Warmth is important, and cosiness, which is why I love fireplaces, candles, music and cushions. Having lived in our current house both as a renter and as an owner, I'm not sure it has felt very different, although choosing curtains and painting our room has felt good. I always pretended all the rented places were ours anyway. A very important part of home for me is the continuity of the generations – a sense not only of physical place and geography but of where we fit in history; so the grand-kids' and kids' pictures and homemade gifts, Mum's desk and Dad's clock, my grandmother's chest and great-grandmother's bureau, all speak of being situated in something bigger and wider and deeper than my own relatively brief appearance on the stage.

Awkward questions

As I've been exploring this idea of house as home, I've had a persistent niggle. When you consider middle-class Western aspirations regarding property in light of the way people live in other places around the globe, or at other times in history, it all looks kind of crazy. I'm thinking about the time Shawn and I took a group of teens from Canada to build houses for families in Juarez, Mexico. We built a house every day, which would sound impressive if you didn't know that a house there consti-tuted four wooden walls and a corrugated-iron roof. These incredibly basic one-room dwellings were received with joy and gratitude by people for whom they represented a significant upgrade. I'm thinking about my friend Julia's grandparents, who raised their family in one room in a Moscow apartment shared by three other families. I'm picturing the teachers' accommodation at Mkwabene Primary School in Zimbabwe where I was on my gap year – a bare concrete shell that was still highly superior to the mud huts the pupils lived in.

Even here in London in the present day, there are many people living in appalling conditions. Joe Peduzzi, a twenty-two-year-old house-hunting for somewhere affordable within reach of his new job, was stunned to find himself being shown a garden shed set up inside a communal living room, being let for £530 per month.[3] Property prices in the capital have led to ingenious uses of space and there are plenty of stories of people living in cupboards under stairs, hallways and unconverted lofts.

Given the huge problems in the world and Jesus' command in the Sermon on the Mount that we not store up treasure on earth, it is worth raising the question of whether Christians should in good conscience invest so much both financially and emotionally in property. Is wholehearted faith compatible with a life devoted to climbing rung by rung up the housing ladder? Is it OK to spend so much of our free time and disposable income making our houses more and more comfortable and stylish? Shouldn't people of faith have a different vision for their accommodation than merely to turn it into their own personal sanctuary, decorated in the aforementioned soothing, textured neutrals? And is it wrong for people who aspire to trust in God to find such a sense of security from a building? Those are really uncomfortable questions, and I think all of us need to answer them for ourselves, being mindful that Jesus was more concerned with the heart of each of his followers than with laying down blanket principles.

Some of us in the world, including me, are living in

unprecedented comfort and stability; we've come to see our luxurious circumstances as normal, not the rare good fortune they are. It is easy to be ungrateful and unappreciative, when all of us with a roof over our head have much to be thankful for. We might have one fewer bedroom than we'd really like, noisy neighbours or a north-facing garden – but if we have somewhere safe and warm to live, we are the lucky ones. Bombing in Syria has razed the ancient city of Aleppo to the ground, leaving hundreds of thousands homeless. Pretty much the whole town of Amatrice in Italy was reduced to rubble by an earthquake in the summer of 2016. In October of the same year, Hurricane Matthew hit Haiti, destroying an estimated 90 per cent of homes on the southern half of the island.[4] Housing everywhere may be vulnerable to flooding, foreclosure, subsidence and woodworm.

I have never faced the trauma of having my home destroyed, and I don't know how I would handle it. A situation like that shows you what you really value, who and what you trust. I would love to think I'd respond like James, a contact I've made through work. This is what he wrote in a recent email:

Dear Jo,

Sorry for the delayed response – we had a house fire so life has been a bit disrupted. All OK though fortunately! It was awful but God has been amazing and put people there to help us at just the right time. No one was hurt but we do have to move out of our

house for a few months. Never mind: we are thankful
for having a rented house.
Hope you are all well,
James

David's dream house

We don't have any biblical description of the house David
grew up in but, thanks to the painstaking work of archae-
ologists, we can make some reasonable assumptions based
on the era and location as well as the size and occupation
of his family. It likely had stone foundations and walls
of stone, mud and straw. The inner walls were probably
finished with clay or plaster and were possibly decorated
with simple frescoes. His house might well have consisted
of a number of small rooms arranged around a courtyard,
with a flat roof used for sleeping in the hotter months,
as well as for drying food and textiles. Food would have
been cooked over a fire in the courtyard. The rooms would
have been small and dark, as windows were scarce, and
furniture minimal: stuffed mats to sit and sleep on, storage
shelves built into the walls. There might have been a stone
bench or two. As soon as David was old enough, he was
sent off with the family flocks and from then on would
have spent little time under his parents' roof.

After living in Saul's court and then spending years on
the move as a fugitive, I imagine it was a huge relief for
David to finally have somewhere to hang his hat, so to
speak. We read 1 Chronicles that when he first arrived in

Jerusalem he took up residence in the fortress as work started on building up the city. David began to have great success as a king, a warrior and a leader, becoming more and more powerful. This was seen by his people, his enemies and by David himself as a sign of God's favour on him: 'The LORD Almighty was with him.'[5]

Somewhat surprisingly, it wasn't David who instigated the building of his palace. According to Chronicles, one day a great caravan of people and animals was seen approaching Jerusalem. It must have been quite a sight in times when transporting anything of significant size was a rare and logistically challenging occurrence. Here were vast cedar logs, the like of which were unknown in Israel, wending their way from Tyre – homage from King Hiram, along with the craftsmen who would know what to do with them. Did David rub his hands together with glee at the prospect of getting his very own fancy palace? Apparently not. He was more interested by the fact that his impressive new living quarters would send a message. He knew this palace wasn't about him at all: 'David knew that the LORD had established him as king over Israel and that his kingdom had been highly exalted for the sake of his people Israel.'[6] David lived in that palace for the rest of his life, but he never wrote a love song about it, although he wrote a lot of songs. The only place that features in his psalms is the 'house of the LORD' – his place of worship – and that's where he seems to really feel at home.

I have lived in a lot of houses, and the degree to which they were each 'home' varied considerably. Our first home in Chalfont St Peter, for all its shortcomings, taught me to knuckle down and properly inhabit my surroundings. Our next house gave me a glimpse of how a lovely house can make life lovely, but also the value of holding on to good gifts lightly. The building where we sleep, keep our stuff, have a legal right to be and where we have legal obligations to fulfil, is not incidental to the idea of home. But a building will never be all there is to home. Our dwelling place is only one facet; just as important are our people, our community, and that's where we're going next.

CHAPTER TEN

Care in the community

My church is my home

St James, Gerrards Cross

*People come to a church longing for, yearning for,
hoping for this sense of roots, place, belonging,
sharing and caring. People come to a church in our
time with a search for community.*[1]
     Kennon L. Callahan, *Effective Church Leadership*

AS MUCH AS anything else, home means people. For all but
the most extreme introverts, the nicest house in the world
won't cut it if you live there in splendid isolation; setting
the table for one, night after night, is a bleak activity, no
matter how fine the bone china. And by people, I don't
mean only close family. I mean whoever is a part of our

community. Community can be an elusive concept, but we all know when we've found one. You might be part of a community at your gym, or in your street, or at your woodworking club. A community is a group of people with something in common; it is those we live and work alongside, those who share our values or who care about the same things. We are made to belong in these groups, and when we do, we find home within them.

A few weeks ago, Shawn had a rare Sunday off, so we decided to visit another church. As we walked in, we were greeted by smiling people who said, 'Welcome home!' They couldn't have known we belonged to another church and that this wasn't our home, but it made me feel warm inside regardless. For Christians, church can be – hopefully it often is – home.

People talk about the church as a broken institution, one that bears only the faintest resemblance to the church described in the biblical book of Acts, which shared life, transformed society around it, lived and died to be like Jesus. They (and perhaps you) distrust its hierarchies, call out its hypocrisies and yawn at its traditions. You don't need to be part of a church to worship God, the argument goes. You can worship God anywhere. You can build community and give of your time, skills and money to make the world better, and you can read the Bible on your own, so what is church for?

I'm sure there are those of you who relate to these impressions and ask these questions. Perhaps you have a gut-level uneasiness about finding a chapter on church in a book about home. For some of you it may trigger real pain, because maybe at one time you hoped church would be a home and now you've let go of those dreams. But there will also be those of you for whom church has been a lifeline, the first and only place you've been both known and loved, a sign of hope in a fragmented world. The church is not a human invention; it was founded by Jesus Christ himself, and it is because of him that, together, we who form the church are more than the sum of our parts.

In which I leave church and then come back

If our nine years in Chalfont St Peter were an experiment in searching for home in a neighbourhood and a house, they were also a revelation in terms of discovering home in a church. Being at home in church took me by surprise; it caught me out and far exceeded my low expectations. Let me explain.

I have happy memories of the church where my dad served as a curate after ordination. It was somewhere I felt safe and known. When we came back from Portugal to visit, it was nice to be surrounded by a host of warm, smiley people who remembered me from when I was a pre-schooler and who had evidently been keeping tabs on our family and praying for us. But I didn't think of it as a home-like place, because we were visitors, albeit visitors with a historical claim.

In my early life my most vivid encounters with God happened outside: on a beach, in a dusty pine wood, on a windy hilltop. The weekly get-togethers at Cruzinha had many of the elements of a traditional church service – sung worship, preaching, prayer, communion – but our community was in constant flux, a revolving door of new faces. Then there was chapel at boarding school, five hundred people in the pews every Sunday, but only because there were penalties if you didn't show up. At university I went to two different churches, but I was so busy doing things with the campus Christian Union that I didn't have time to get to know anyone at church, let alone help out, or 'serve', to use the correct religious terminology. During my first two years in Vancouver I went to church, but grudgingly. We had college chapel on Tuesdays, I spent pretty much all my time with Christians learning about Christian things and, when not studying, I worked in a Christian bookstore. I decided I had quite enough Christian activity in my weekly routine, and I quit church. As I explained to Shawn at the time, I understood church as the body of Christ, the worldwide community of all disciples, and I wasn't amputating myself. I was still a committed finger, or toe, or whatever I was, but I would now be spending Sundays doing as I pleased. Shawn's response – an expression of shock and sadness, followed by a reasoned defence of committed membership of a local congregation – began a slow change of my resistant heart. But St James in Gerrards Cross was my first lived experience of being fully part of a church.

St James is a thriving parish church. There are multiple services every Sunday, and each of them has its own distinctive character, ranging from the more formal organ-and-Book-of-Common-Prayer-type affair, to the jolly family-friendly celebration, to the contemporary-style evening get-together. As churches in the UK go, St James had a fairly large membership. Big churches have plenty of advantages, but one of the downsides is that with all those people it can be hard to feel you are anything other than a face in the crowd. As the spouse of someone on staff, you might think I had more of a chance of being recognised, but it didn't always work that way. St James had a church centre that was open throughout the week. The staff offices were on the first floor, and if you wanted to go up to see a staff member, your husband for example, you had to get past the eagle-eyed volunteers on the welcome desk. After we'd been there for six years, I made the mistake of thinking I could breeze past with a smile and a wave, and head on up. 'Excuse me,' came an anxious voice from behind me the first time I tried this. A deceptively fragile-looking octogenarian in a lilac cardigan and pearls was hurrying after me. 'You can't go up there, I'm afraid. That's where the staff work.' She stepped in front of me, blocking the stairway in case I hadn't fully got the message, and glanced over at her two colleagues on the desk for backup.

'It's OK,' I said. 'I'm Shawn's wife – he's expecting me.' She looked me up and down doubtfully.

'We want to see Daddy,' three-year-old Alexa said. She ducked around the zealous welcomer-cum-guard-dog and scuttled up the stairs, calling out airily over her shoulder, 'Bye Bunchies!'

'Bunchies?' I asked when I caught her up.

'I don't know their names so I call them the bunchies,'

she explained. They might not have known who we were, but we didn't know them either. That wouldn't have been the case in a smaller church.

Settling in to St James had its rocky moments, and not just because of its size. In an effort to get to know some people, I joined a group of women from the church who met for coffee and a discussion about the Bible once a week. Shortly after I arrived, the group put on an event to raise money to dig a well in Africa. I didn't have the mandatory Le Creuset casserole dish from which to serve the food we were all supposed to cook, the ingredients for which I couldn't afford, and I spent the evening burning with shame about my shabby charity shop outfit and inappropriate footwear.

In many ways this church and I were not a natural fit. It had an emphasis on doing things to a high standard, aiming for excellence in all things, whereas I'm more of a 'good enough will do' sort of person. The area covered by its parish was affluent, and many in the congregation were prosperous; Shawn and I, meanwhile, had student debt, and no savings or assets. While we aimed to one day get into the black, we had no particular desire to become wealthy. It wasn't common for people to cry in public, something I do often, or wander around without their shoes on, as I've been known to do. Pretty much everyone was English and assumed, unhelpfully if not exactly incorrectly, that I was too, and as a childless twenty-something I was a demographic anomaly.

For some people this cultural mismatch would have been too much. As a staff wife, though, I didn't feel I had the freedom to shop around for somewhere more comfortable, and in the end I'm so glad I didn't.

I'm not sure when I began to feel as though this was my place and these were my people, but I did. I knew I was different in so many ways, but mostly all I encountered was acceptance and love, and eventually, after weeks of reluctantly showing up from a sense of duty, I discovered that, against all the odds, I belonged.

I've thought about what stories I could tell you to express the way St James became a home to me. There are many to choose from. In the end I've landed on the time around Alexa's birth, when we'd been at St James for three years. I'd wanted to be a mother for a very long time, was in a job I was very happy to leave, and I'd read a book which laid out all you needed to know to make sure your baby slept like a log and not like a baby. What could possibly go wrong?

My gorgeous, healthy daughter came into the world ten days early but without complications, beyond the fact that no one had sent me the nesting memo and her bassinet was buried under a heap of junk in the box room. She was perfect and I loved her, but she didn't get along with the principles of sleep management I tried to teach her, feeding was painful for both of us, and I was overwhelmed by the sense I had lost myself and all trace of life as I'd known it.

Shawn was working six days a week and studying for ordination, and my parents, while loving and supportive, lived in another country. I would have been in trouble if it hadn't been for church. Church was somewhere I could turn up, pasty-faced and deranged, in maternity clothing that still felt a little tight around the waist. Church was somewhere a hundred pairs of hands would reach out to take the bundle from my arms and give me a break. Church was the people who brought meals around night after night, who kitted us out with every bit of equipment and clothing we needed, who were happy to talk to me over high-volume squalling, and who let me come to their houses and sleep while they took over jiggling duties. Church was where I was reminded that God is always present, regardless of what our emotions say; that he is good and loving and powerful and to be worshipped. Church was where I heard Scripture read, and explained and applied in simple enough terms that even my tired brain could absorb it. And it was a place I felt I could bless others, in however limited a way, and mostly, in the early days, by drinking tea with girls from the youth group and absorbing their angst about boys, exams and thigh circumference. St James was my community, and it was my home.

The heart of the home

In January 2013, the first meeting of The Sunday Assembly took place in Islington in London. The vision of two comedians who wanted to do church without God, Sunday Assembly meetings involve singing, talks, community building, and the encouragement to do good and make the world a better place. Pippa Evans, one of the founders, had been a Christian at one time; when she stopped believing, those were the things she missed, she said, not God. The group's website says, 'We want the Sunday Assembly to be a place of compassion, where, no matter what your situation, you are welcomed, accepted, and loved.' Since that first meeting, the idea has taken off, and there are now seventy chapters in eight countries. One attendee, Gintare Karalyte, said in an interview with the BBC, 'I think people need that sense of connectedness because everyone is so singular right now; to be part of something, and to feel like you are part of something – that's what people are craving in the world.' The Sunday Assembly clearly meets a need. In an increasingly individualistic, isolating world, it is somewhere to belong. The people it has drawn and enthused have identified a need in themselves for a home that is more than their accommodation, their neighbourhood, their culture and their family.

Pippa identified what she saw as the best characteristics of church and has tried to recreate them to gain the benefits she's missed in her life as an atheist. But the reason church works is that it is built around a man who modelled radical, sacrificial love – a man whose example and continuing presence enables his followers to love each other in the same way. Over his last Passover meal, a few short hours before his death, Jesus talked to his disciples about their communal life when he was no longer physically with them: 'As I have loved you, so you must love one another. By this everyone will know that you are my disciples, if you love one another.'[2] There's something irresistibly compelling about this kind of love when you encounter it. When Christians find home in church, there is a whole other dimension to what that means. What we discover is that together we share home with God himself.[3] The Canadian Catholic philosopher, theologian and founder of the L'Arche movement, Jean Vanier, writes: 'Communities of students or friends who come together for a short time can be signs of hope. But the communities whose members live faithfully a life-long covenant with God, among themselves and with the poor, are more important still. They are signs of the fidelity of God.'[4]

It is slightly hard to nail down what church is, exactly. It has little intrinsically to do with meeting in a building with a spire, or on a Sunday, or being led by someone in fancy ecclesiastical clothing, and there is a lot more to it than songs, talks and fuzzy warm feelings of belonging. So what are its defining features? To answer that, perhaps it would help us to go back to the beginning.

The opening chapters of Genesis tell of a time when God enjoyed comfortable companionship with Adam and Eve. The intimacy of Eden came to an abrupt end as the temptation to eat from the tree of knowledge of good and evil proved too strong. A deep fracture had formed in humankind's relationship with God; Adam and Eve were banished – thrown out of their first home and out of God's holy presence. But while a certain closeness was lost, it wasn't the end of the divine–human relationship. The church is first and foremost a gathering of people among whom God is present, and by whom God is worshipped. From the very beginning, humanity has needed and desired community both with each other and with God, and yet has sabotaged both at every turn.

After Adam and Eve had left the garden, it didn't take long for the first murder to occur, and by the time of Noah 'every inclination of the thoughts of the human heart was only evil all the time' (Genesis 6:5). From this mess, one family and a host of animals were salvaged on Noah's ark, and God made a covenant with them and with the earth itself – a binding agreement involving obligations on both sides. Around four hundred years later, God spoke to a man called Abraham, telling him he was to be the father of a nation chosen to be blessed by God and to be a blessing to all people. Abraham and his wife Sarah were childless and elderly, but in fulfilment of God's promise they conceived a son, Isaac. Isaac was Jacob's father, and Jacob was Joseph's. Joseph was sold by his brothers, who were jealous of his spectacular coat and the favouritism it signified, and ended up in Egypt, where his skills in dream interpretation landed him a peachy government job. When famine brought the rest of the family to seek aid, they were reunited and settled in Egypt, where they flourished, in time becoming 'so numerous that the land was filled with them' (Exodus 1:7). They were slaves for centuries, until God enacted a dramatic rescue.

What followed was decades in the desert, learning what it meant to be a worshipping community, a 'kingdom of priests and a holy nation' (Exodus 19:6). Moses would meet with God at the top of Mount Sinai, then instruct the people about what was expected of them. A chest was built, known as the ark of the covenant, and in it were kept the stone tablets inscribed with the Ten Commandments. The ark lived in the tabernacle, a sanctuary in which God's presence would dwell. The tabernacle was hugely significant – the focal point of Israel's worship, and the tangible sign that God was with them. When Israel crossed the Jordan to fight for their promised land, the ark went before them. With the people established and settled, the ark came to rest first in Bethel and then in Shiloh where the prophet Samuel lived, from Shiloh to Philistine country for a few miserable months when Saul messed up, and then to the town of Kiriath Jearim for twenty years.

So after that whistle-stop tour, here we are at David's place in history, with hopefully some feeling for how the ark was both a symbol of God's presence and, in some mysterious sense, the place where his presence rested in a literal way.

David wouldn't have understood the idea of choosing or rejecting membership of a religious community. He was born into a race that knew itself chosen by God. In their not-so-distant past, God had rescued them from Egypt. He had made his dwelling place on earth in their midst. We know from the Psalms that David had a sense of awe and gratitude about worshipping God: 'I, by your great love, can come into your house; in reverence I bow down towards your holy temple' (Psalm 5:7).

When Jerusalem became the capital city of the united kingdoms of Israel and Judah, it made sense to bring the ark there. With great ceremony and celebration, David and thirty thousand others went to collect it and transport it to its new home. However, rather than following the very specific instructions, which God had given through Moses, about how it should be carried, they loaded it onto an ox cart. The oxen stumbled, the ark nearly fell off, and a man called Uzziah reached out and grabbed it so it wouldn't fall on the ground. Uzziah was immediately struck down dead by God for his 'irreverent act'.[5] This episode was hard to stomach for David, who got very angry. But it is perhaps even harder for us who, generally speaking, take worship and church very lightly.

After three months, David gave it another go, and this time all proper obeisance was shown to the ark. As it arrived in the city, David danced and leapt before it, offering sacrifices and worshipping God with everything he was. Commissioning Asaph as chief worship leader, he said, 'Great is the Lord and most worthy of praise . . . Splendour and majesty are before him; strength and joy are in his dwelling place' (1 Chronicles 16:25, 27).

Unlike David, we have the assurance of God's Spirit making his home in each one of us who makes him welcome. Believers have replaced the ark and the tabernacle. As Paul writes to the church in Corinth, 'Don't you know that you yourselves are God's temple and that God's Spirit lives among you?'[6]

Our English word 'church' comes from the Greek *ekklesia,* literally meaning 'an assembly', or 'called-out ones'. As children of God, all believers are by default part of the same family. Of course you can be part of a family and have nothing to do with anyone else in it, or decide to only spend time with the one sibling who really gets you and shares your love of thimble-collecting, or redefine family to mean the whole human race and therefore absolve yourself of the need to go to family get-togethers. But if you do, both you and your family will be worse off. When we are fully engaged participating members of our church families, our skills, resources and company will bless other people (and it feels good to be needed). We will find that in hard times we are carried and supported. When our faith is weak and doubts creep in, we'll draw strength from seeing those around us staying firm.

In a letter to the church in Rome, Paul writes, 'For just as each of us has one body with many members . . . so in Christ we, though many, form one body, and each member belongs to all the others' (Romans 12:4–5). Knowing we belong is a huge part of what it means to be at home in a church. No church is perfect, and throwing in your lot with a group of people whose only commonality is who they worship is very uncomfortable and awkward. But for a Christian, church is supposed to be a home. I haven't given up on that idea. I hope and pray you haven't either.

CHAPTER ELEVEN

What do you do?
My work is my home

Where our work is, there let our joy be.

Tertullian

THOSE LIVING IN wealthy, peaceful societies often pursue an idea of fulfilment in work: a job that somehow reflects the essence of who we are; one that we believe in and do for reasons above and beyond the fact that we have bills to pay and mouths to feed. Frederick Buechner defines vocation as 'the place where your deep gladness meets the world's deep need'.[1] What a beautiful place to find. In his book *Let Your Life Speak: Listening for the Voice of Vocation*, the writer, teacher and activist Parker J. Palmer urges us to first discover who we are, and let that then shape what we do: 'The deepest vocational question is not, "What ought I to do with my life?" It is the more elemental and demanding "Who am I? What is my nature?"'[2] Who could argue with the wisdom of that sentiment? And yet it makes me feel wary.

I'm wary for several reasons. First, few in this broken world have the luxury of indulging in the exercise of introspection. If we think back to Maslow's pyramid of needs, only those with immense good fortune are free to seek self-actualisation. Does that mean the blessed among us – those who can – shouldn't? No; but I think it's worth being aware that alignment between our toil and our nature is a rare privilege.

Second, thinking about work in terms of vocation hints at a hierarchy – some forms of employment deemed more meaningful and valuable than others. What jobs come to mind when you consider vocation? My mind begins to swim with priests, artists, teachers and doctors. I've never met a client data and management information coordinator or a ledger control assistant with a particular sense of calling, or a child who dreams of working for the council fixing potholes when they grow up, but these are worthy and necessary roles.

Third, I am wary of the notion of vocation because I think the very concept can lead to discontentment, a tendency to crane towards a misty point on the horizon where lieth 'What I Am Supposed To Do With My Life'. Annie Dillard wrote, 'How we spend our days is, of course, how we spend our lives.'[3] Every minute counts, not just those minutes spent in our most glorious employment.

And fourth, I worry that thinking of our work as a vocation, not a job, somehow justifies an unhealthy tendency towards workaholism, all other problems becoming subsumed by our calling. There are numerous sad stories of people who have accomplished incredible things in their work life at the expense of their marriage, family, friendships and their own physical and mental health. I've had friends who have talked about their husband or wife living at the office. They are there morning until night, and even when they walk through the door of their homes, grey with exhaustion, their minds are occupied elsewhere. There is nothing intrinsically wrong with long hours and hard work, but it's dangerous to neglect other dimensions of life.

Work plays a significant part in the life of the majority of adults. The story of creation in the book of Genesis tells us we were made to spend six of seven days expending energy and effort on necessary tasks. By and large work is a good thing, and where we work and what we do plays an important part in whether or not we feel at home in our lives as a whole. A home at-work is about more than the physical space we spend our time in; it is about the security and familiarity it offers.

Conversely, for those still looking for direction, unsure where or what they should be doing, or who are unemployed, life can feel unsettled, a bit like 'sofa-surfing', where people have no permanent address and move between friends' homes. And when a role is abruptly terminated, whether due to redundancy, health issues or dismissal, it can seem like an eviction. You are suddenly unsure where to be or even who you are.

Job hunting

The whole concept of finding a career overshadowed my teens. Growing up with parents who'd built a charity from scratch based on passionate conviction and a clear sense of calling was inspiring, but also intimidating and inhibitive. Watching them and trying to deduce replicable principles, I became more and more disheartened. What on earth could I do that would impact the world for good, allow me to experience the good things in life even if the pay was low, tie together my interests and my skills (especially as I wasn't entirely sure what skills I had to offer) – and preferably allow me to live in a hot climate near a beach?

When I was fourteen my school gave everyone a career test. The test asked several hundred probing questions, including gems such as, 'Do you enjoy talking about rocks with your friends?' and, 'Do you get excited about comic books?' The computer analysed my answers and spat out the suggestion that I become a probation officer or shop-window dresser. I had been thinking more along the lines of a missionary-journalist (my own invention), or perhaps a psychologist. The psychology idea was put to bed once I was told there was a mathematical component to the degree I would need to get, and journalism seemed a very competitive field, in which I couldn't imagine finding success. Maybe, I concluded, I would just have to marry someone with clear goals and tag along in a supportive capacity. So I chose my university studies based on what sounded interesting rather than what would be useful, and hoped things would fall into place at some point.

My first experience of employment was gruesome. At the beginning of the summer holidays after my first year at university, I went to stay with a friend in London, printed out a pile of CVs (I've never found it harder to fill a side of A4 before or since) and pounded the streets begging for work. After several days, I was taken on by a café on upmarket Hampstead High Street for £2 per hour, a rate I was assured would rise to a very respectable wage with all the tips that would come rolling in. I broke glasses, confused orders, asked the parents of a little girl if their son would like a straw for his drink, and was fired on my third shift having not received a single tip. I sat in the staff room with aching feet and a splitting headache, and cried with shame.

I went back to Birmingham soon after and joined a temp agency, which sent me to the children's hospital to do two weeks of filing in the basement. That led to three summers spent in a variety of hospital admin roles, from working on Reception in Heart Investigations, to covering in Social Services for a medical secretary on sick leave, to acting as PA for a hospital manager. I can't say I loved it, but I became great friends with my colleagues; when I left for the last time they threw me a huge goodbye party and showered me with gifts. (Mostly make-up. My bare-faced approach to life worried them.) I began to see that meaning in work didn't come only from the specific tasks you did, but from relating to the people doing those tasks alongside you. I also learned that working hard and doing menial but necessary roles is profoundly honourable.

As you already know, I didn't get a full-time job on graduation, but deferred that challenge by doing more study. Alongside my studies I did have various part-time jobs: I worked in the college bookstore, I was a nanny for a gorgeous little boy with cerebral palsy, I was a teaching assistant for two Regent professors, I ran a church crèche and I did cleaning, gardening and babysitting. When my studies were done, Shawn had another year to go, so I worked part-time as a receptionist and did an internship as a hospital chaplain.

By the time we moved back to England, I had fixed upon the idea of hospital chaplaincy as the way ahead, but as soon as I began to look into it properly, I realised I would need to be ordained. Having just finished a theology degree, I was not at all inspired by the idea of more study and, after a couple of meetings with an Anglican vocations advisor, I withdrew from the selection process. I would have been quite happy at that point to see if we could have a baby, but we had huge student loans and we decided we should have a run at paying them off first.

I was not at all sure what my experience or education qualified me to do, so I just looked around for who was hiring in the locality. The Epilepsy Society was just over the other side of the village and I applied for a care-worker vacancy. Care workers are not highly valued in our society, but oh my goodness, they should be. I was at the Epilepsy Society for three years, until Alexa was born, working to enable adults with learning difficulties and uncontrolled seizures to live the best lives possible. It was often boring and menial; I had close contact with every bodily fluid a human can produce; I was held hostage at knife-point by a resident who'd grown a little possessive of me; I came alongside deep suffering and brokenness and was confronted by my own ugliness and limitations on a daily basis. I was also loved in a wholehearted and uncomplicated way, and I formed lasting friendships with fellow staff members.

One of the strange aspects of this job was that I was working in the residents' homes, spending time in their kitchens, bedrooms and bathrooms; being paid to intrude on their most domestic, intimate moments. Another of its challenges was a persistent feeling that while I was trying hard to make the best of the situation, it wasn't really what I wanted to be doing with my life. After a year, I landed my first book contract and began writing in my spare time, and that creative, intellectual outlet was a lifeline. I have to admit too that on occasions when I felt insecure or ashamed that I wasn't doing something more conventionally successful, I'd add, 'I'm writing my first book too,' hoping they'd infer there would be other books to come.

Signing that first book contract was a mountaintop experience and, for a few glorious hours, I believed it would change my life beyond all recognition. However, as any author who isn't Stephen King or Philip Yancey will tell you, one book does not a fulfilled and lucrative writing life create. Far from it. I wrote the book, and on turning it in I was offered a second contract. Delivery of book two coincided with delivery of baby one, and she took all my attention. Unable to do much by way of introducing the book to the world, I naively assumed it would be found by eager readers regardless, and enthusiastically passed on to their friends. When sales figures for that second book proved dismally low, the publishers cut me loose. I was devastated. I had set my heart on being a writer, I thought I had figured out how it would fit around motherhood, and I had no plan B.

Around that time I went for coffee with a lady at church, Caroline, who was a freelance writer for various Christian publications. She talked me step by step through how to do an article pitch, outlined which magazines liked what sort of content and suggested I get into writing daily Bible notes, offering to introduce me to her editor. From that conversation, a new direction began to emerge, and bit by bit I picked up work. A third, fourth and fifth book followed, written in scraps of time mined like precious metal from my densely packed domestic responsibilities.

Times changed dramatically in book publishing over the years I was writing. The organisation that had published my last three books proceeded to more or less shut its publishing arm, and once again I had to find a new home for my words. The tougher new commercial world was looking for profile, platform and the reliable prospect of sales. Authors who wanted their books in print had to be willing to know their brand and sell their work. Everything in me rebelled at the idea of becoming a marketing machine for my own products, and yet I badly wanted to keep writing. A meeting with a commissioning editor in November 2013 crystallised the choice before me and I went home miserable and paralysed with indecision. I didn't want to work at becoming famous. But I did want to be a writer.

We had just moved to Surbiton, and I had a pile of freelance work to keep me going. I delayed the process of pitching a new book, all the while chuntering away to myself about the world going to hell in a handcart and the best thing being to give up. I was still under the apprehension that I was otherwise unemployable, but one day while frittering away time doing semi-random internet searches, I came across a permanent, part-time, home-based job that seemed to be just right for someone who could do the kinds of things I could do. The idea of working for a cause bigger than increasing my own name recognition was enticing. I applied and was hired.

I've now spent almost three years working for the Leaders of Worship and Preachers Trust, during which time I've been able to dream up and edit a brand-new magazine, *Preach*, run a grant scheme, forge partnerships with organisations doing things to support preachers in the UK, and collaborate on all kinds of preacher-training initiatives. It has been a wonderful job (although, like most jobs, it has had its terrible moments). And, as you can see from the book you hold in your hand, I've not given up writing.

On a fairly regular basis I become fretful and restless about where I'm going in my work life: what is the next thing, am I doing what I should be with my time and effort, am I challenged enough or too challenged, what is my ten-year plan and what will I do when I finally grow up? When this happens, I remember the old woman who lived in the shoe. It would be a mistake to be so focused on an upgrade that I fail to appreciate the work-home I've already found.

Shepherd, musician, soldier, king

David began his work life with responsibility for the family flocks. The job of tending the family's sheep usually belonged to the youngest; as each child got old enough they would take over the sheep, and the next oldest would start helping their father with the crops. After four hundred years among an Egyptian society that despised shepherding as a menial and uncouth occupation, it wasn't a highly regarded role in Israel, although its status received a boost once this particular sheep-herder became a monarch. And it became one of the most powerful metaphors for God's dealings with humankind in the Bible.

And then, one day, David was called in from the fields to be anointed by a priest as future king of Israel. In a biblical context, the physical act of anointing, a swipe of oil on the forehead, symbolised being chosen and equipped by God for a specific task. David was given the job of ruling God's people, but first he had to work for another anointed king. Saul's kingship was no longer an outworking of his anointing, but an almighty effort to be a good ruler under his own steam. Despite this, David had too much respect for God's clear initial call on Saul to even think about staging a coup. And so, for twenty years, David lived with the identity and calling of a king without doing the work of a king, and for the first few he was essentially Saul's servant, first in the capacity of musician and then as a soldier. It must have been frustrating and frightening, like treading water in treacherous rapids, but David remained for the most part focused and dignified. Even in his years in the wilderness, he didn't lose his identity or his work ethic. He led and shepherded the motley crowd on the run with him, and provided protection to flocks of animals vulnerable to bandits.

Once he was crowned ruler over Judah and then Israel, there wasn't the sense of climax or culmination you might expect after all these years of build-up. Life is not like a movie, the screen freezing for a final shot at the moment the story has been progressing towards. David kept working. The peaks and troughs of glorious accomplishment and abject personal failure spooled onwards. Overall, he was a good king. And then he got old and died.

David's work was the primary context in which his spirituality played out. His identity was profoundly shaped by his God-given calling to be a king. But he always made his home in a larger reality, and he always understood his work as an expression of worship to the one who holds all things together:

When I consider your heavens,
the work of your fingers,
the moon and the stars,
which you have set in place,
what is mankind that you are mindful of them,
human beings that you care for them?

You have made them a little lower than the angels
and crowned them with glory and honour.
You made them rulers over the works of your hands;
you put everything under their feet.

(Psalm 8:3–6)

What we can learn from my friend Justin

This week we have a friend from Regent days staying. We've not seen each other in thirteen years, and although we've followed each other's lives at a distance, there's been plenty of catching up to do. The reason Justin is over in England from the US is that he's recently become the sales director for a large Christian publisher out there. I was struck that although he's only been in the role for a year, he talks about his company with possessive pronouns. He has a strong sense of belonging, even ownership. He has an intuitive understanding of the organisational culture, and it's a culture that has an uncanny synergy with his values, character and history. This is someone at home in his work, and I wanted to mine his experience and pass on to you his reflections on the road that's brought him to this place.

Justin's father was a second-generation immigrant from Sweden and was raised in an atmosphere of anxious determination to succeed in the New World. Life needed to be rebuilt from the ground up, and the family worked relentlessly hard. Justin thinks his father would have made a very happy park ranger, but that would never have been acceptable to his parents; instead he became a miserable lawyer. Observing the misery, Justin concluded that no one in their right mind would choose to work in a business environment.

Justin's first plan was to become a history teacher, and in college he majored in history. But it was the theology classes he took on the side that captured his imagination, and so he changed track, deciding he would become a theologian. To this end he arrived at Regent to do his Masters, where we met. He applied for a role in the college bookstore, thinking he would be a general dogsbody, like me – and to his surprise he was offered a full-time management role.

However carefully we might try to craft the shape of our lives, so much seems to turn on happenstance. Was this Justin stumbling unawares on 'God's Plan for His Life'? I really don't know, although I'm someone who doesn't generally think in terms of God's plan involving a carefully worked out, step-by-step career progression. Think of how many faithful, good people spend their lives slaving away in coleslaw factories or unable to work after a run-in with farm machinery. I can't believe God planned things so that millions of highly skilled Syrians would find themselves having a midlife vocational upheaval and slaving at anything that offers a possible way to survive. Christians look for, and often find, the fingerprints of God's provision, goodness and kindness in every aspect of their lives. But I would argue there is no divinely perfect job blueprint out there for us to find.

Back to Justin: working at the bookstore taught him that a life in business didn't have to equate to meaningless misery, and he began to rethink some of his work-related assumptions. Once he and his wife Joy had graduated, they moved back to the United States. Justin was employed as a copywriter for a publisher, and was swiftly promoted to publicist. While in many ways this seems as if it ought to be a high point of the career story, it was a difficult two years. So much about whether or not we feel a sense of home in our work-life is about the people we work alongside. You can be working for an organisation you admire, filling your days with meaningful and varied tasks, in a beautiful, light and well-organised environment and still feel you don't fit, aren't welcome, don't belong, if the people don't become your people. The publishing house was a family business with a long and prestigious history, but resistant to change and rigidly hierarchical. Justin's ideas weren't welcome and he felt stifled. It became clear to him that the institutional dysfunction was too deeply entrenched for him to impact for good, and when he saw a vacancy as a book-buyer for a university bookstore in the same town, he applied. The role was to oversee sales of everything that wasn't required reading for the various student courses, and while some might not have seen the potential, and friends questioned the wisdom of what

seemed like a step down, Justin took his area of responsibility and ran it like a kingdom of endless possibility.
He didn't see himself as just a buyer of books, but as
someone with the opportunity to shape culture. He was
in the business of thought leadership.

I can't tell you how much I love that perspective. There
is something profoundly exciting about blowing apart the
pre-conceived parameters of your given job description
and making the very most of where you are. Perhaps you
don't have a glamorous title, but I wonder what you could
do with the job you have in order to leverage your
God-given skills for the good of your workplace, and the
world? Justin not only doubled sales from his department
in a year, he cultivated a new excitement about books on
campus. He got students and faculty meeting together in
book groups, organised life-changing trips such as the
'Food and Faith' adventure, which saw them working on
a pecan farm and drinking tea with the great Wendell
Berry himself, and carefully curated the books on sale in
his store so that his customers would be nourished with
the very best thinking and writing in print.

After years of working in Christian bookstores, Justin
decided to do an MBA, with the thought that he would
maybe branch into the mainstream book world. But having
finished, he found it hard to find work. Several hopeful-
seeming opportunities closed down one by one. One in
particular seemed a perfect fit. The recruitment process
took three months, and when the job went to someone
else, he went into mourning.

If a job is a facet of home, being out of work is a form

of homelessness; I'm pretty sure anyone who's experienced unemployment will resonate with that. Justin was
in his home country, living in a house he owned with his
wife and two little children, in a city he loved, a member
of a thriving church. And yet the struggle of being out of
work was about more than financial pressure. It was a
matter of home, of belonging, of identity. Few of us have
a trouble-free ride through the world of work. Whether
it's periods of unemployment, taking on unskilled work
from desperation, working under bullying bosses or with
colleagues who annoy you or in an office with no daylight,
or having to work several jobs to make ends meet: who
hasn't got these stories to throw into the mix when the
subject comes around at the pub or over a coffee? These
situations unsettle us to our core because as adults we
hope and expect to find our place in the world of work.
But they are also opportunities to test our resilience and
to strengthen and broaden our understanding of home so
that work doesn't need to be everything.

After six months spent fruitlessly applying for job after
job, Justin took a position behind the tills in the local
Barnes and Noble. In many ways it was a dark year, but
it wasn't wasted time. Without the prop of a shiny and
all-consuming career, pain and fragility emerged that he
had always been able to avoid, and once it was in the
open, he had to face it. Reflecting on it now, he says he's
grateful for the chance to be undone and rebuild his life
around a more solid core. Now in what is in many ways
his dream job, he has no illusion that things are always
going to be plain sailing, but he's also clear that his (very

impressive) title does not define him. He's not at a destination. He's not 'completed'.

The biblical picture of heaven reflects all of life, albeit
redeemed and glorious. Work pre-existed the fall: Adam
and Eve had the very demanding task of cultivating the
land, caring for each other and stewarding the animals,
birds and fish. It was no doubt tiring, but as anyone who's
done a hard day of work will know, there is a good kind
of tired that you feel when you've expended your energy
on something wholesome. A good way to make someone
feel at home in a new context is to give them a role to
play, a task to accomplish. I often come and write in a
Surbiton coffee shop called Ex Cellar. When they started
to let me load the dishwasher, it became a home from
home.

When we find work that is satisfying, demanding but
not draining, fruitful and life-enhancing, and done alongside good people, what we are tasting is a foreshadow of
heaven. And what we are experiencing is home.

CHAPTER TWELVE

The story of my life

My past is my home

Newport, Pembrokeshire

The unexamined life is not worth living.

Socrates

HAVING CLUNG LIMPET-LIKE to one place for so long, prising myself away from Chalfont St Peter was a painful process. I wept and moped and fought against the very idea of moving on, coming up with far-fetched scenarios in which we found a way to stay forever. There was excellent provision for the elderly in the Gerrards Cross area, I pleaded. And still room in the St James grave-yard.

But a strange thing happened the day we packed the

final oddments into the car and set off behind the removal van towards Surbiton. I remembered that I knew how to move. Muscle memory kicked in, and suddenly I knew how to handle it. In fact, it was liberating. I'd been suppressing my footloose nature for years, but it was still hard-wired into me. If I had been a dog I would have stuck my head out of the window so the wind blew my ears back, and howled with the exhilaration of a new adventure. Being human, all I did was turn the music up a bit and grin to myself.

We settled fast, here in Surbiton. It felt like home within a matter of days, and although I'd been reminded that moving was in my blood, I was still convinced of the need to commit wholeheartedly to where I was, for however long I was there.

Neither Shawn nor I had even heard of Surbiton before coming across the job advertisement. We'd not seen the classic TV series *The Good Life* that had made its name, and we actually had to look it up on a map. By the time Shawn was applying for jobs, I'd already made my peace with the fact that we would be moving, but at that point I was living in the first house I had loved as an adult, and so I asked God if maybe I could have a fruit tree and a fireplace in our next house (knowing this was a spoilt and audacious thing to ask, but also knowing my generous father God wouldn't mind me asking, as long as I didn't have a tantrum if I didn't get what I wanted). When we were shown around the house on the interview day, the first thing I noticed was the two apple trees in the back garden; the second was the chimney and hearth in the front room. Breathless with excitement, I asked if it was in working order. Sue, our tour guide, went over to have a closer look. 'Well, it's been boarded up, but I don't see why we couldn't try to get it working. If you end up living here,' she added, bringing me back to reality. Once everything was official, Sue remembered my child-like fizzing and got a man to come and inspect the fireplace. The hearth needed extending, the chimney needed lining and ideally a wood-burner should be installed. It would be an expensive job. We didn't have the money for it, and really that should have been the end of the story. But a beautiful wood-burner crackles and spits companionably next to me as I write. An unknown benefactor, hearing that the new associate minister's wife had some kind of emotional attachment to pyrotechnics, donated the necessary funds. It makes me a bit teary even now. There is something about a fire that just says home to me. The smell, the sound, the heat on my cheeks and the chill on the back of my neck, the way it makes the light in the room a playful, dancing presence, the way each fire connects me to other fires in other places.

In the early days in Surbiton, I found myself thinking a lot about my other times and places. When you arrive in a new place, where no one knows you and you know no one, there's a comfort in reminding yourself of the road that brought you here, the people and places that have made you who you are. There's nothing like having to introduce yourself to an entirely new set of people all at the same time to throw your sense of identity into disarray, and a firm grip on your history is a good counterbalance to the chaos.

Times of transition are valuable opportunities to refine your narrative, to step back and search for the coherence in all those moments that add up to your life. All of us have a life story and, as Eugene Peterson says, 'Story is the primary means we have for learning what the world is, and what it means to be a human being in it.' The first piece of work I had to do for my Master's degree at Regent was to write my story. There was a required class called 'The Christian Life'. Half of the weekly three-hour allocation was a lecture, and half was spent in a 'community group'. We were asked to write our life story and then read it out to our group – which, as you might imagine, was pretty frightening. But the process of crafting a piece of shareable writing out of who we were and what we'd done up to that moment was indescribably valuable and, if you haven't before, I would recommend you do it now. And hearing other people's stories when you first meet, rather than the bald facts they would put on bureaucratic forms, sets the tone for your entire relationship.

I'm assuming here a general benevolence towards our past selves, but of course there are those of us who would like nothing more than the possibility of a clean slate. However, as the truism has it: wherever you go, there you are. There is no such thing as a new start. Shawn's great-great-grandfather was an early pioneer in the US, and his story is told in the book *The Exploits of Ben Arnold: Indian Fighter, Gold Miner, Cowboy, Hunter, & Army Scout*.[1] Born into a military family in 1844, he enlisted in the army three times under three different names, deserting each time. The third time he escaped with his life after a mutiny, heading into the wilderness with only a pony, a gun and ten dollars. He operated a ferry, hunted buffalo, fought the Sioux Indians in Crook's campaign in 1876, married an Indian woman and finally died on a homestead in South Dakota in 1922. Ben Arnold not only suffered from acute wanderlust, but had a propensity for rousing people to murderous rage. From choice and necessity he started from scratch multiple times. But he clearly had a desire to pull these disparate chapters into a whole, and at the end of his life he recounted to his daughter the history we are able to read today to his great-great-great-granddaughters.

Brené Brown writes in typically vivid fashion, 'I can't think of a better way to describe what it feels like to get your head and heart around *who you are* and *where you come from* than wrestling a greased pig in the dark. Our identities are always changing and growing, they're not meant to be pinned down. Our histories are never all good or all bad, and running from the past is the surest way to be defined by it.'[2] Making our peace with where we've come from is how we'll be able to find home in the story from here on.

The family tree house

A sense of home comes not just from knowing our own story, but from being able to place our story within bigger stories. In the mid-1990s, an American psychologist, Sara Duke, began to notice that those of her patients who knew the most about their family histories did better in their treatment. At the time her husband, Marshall Duke, was researching myth and ritual in American families at Emory University, and along with a colleague, Robert Fivush, he developed a study to explore her intriguing findings. Children from four dozen families were asked a number of questions about their family history in a 'Do You Know?' test, the results of which were compared to comprehensive psychological assessments. Reporting on the findings in an article for *The New York Times*, Bruce Feiler says, 'The more children knew about their family's history, the stronger their sense of control over their lives, the higher their self-esteem and the more successfully they believed their families functioned. The "Do You Know?" scale turned out to be the best single predictor of children's emotional health and happiness.'[3]

When I moved to North America, one of the first things to strike me as different was the way people answered the question 'Where are you from?' It was fairly standard to reach back several generations for the answer. Joe was not from Nebraska; he was from Ireland and Germany, lands where his great-great-grandparents had been born. Sandra was from Croatia, Racquel from the Philippines and Indonesia, and John's veins ran with pure English blood, no matter that he'd never been there. When we went to Sweden for my uncle's wedding, my Minnesotan husband found himself completely at home. So much of the culture he'd grown up with had, unbeknown to him, been transplanted from this corner of northern Europe. A connection with our history feeds our roots and strengthens our sometimes tenuous hold on where exactly we fit on this planet.

There is now a whole industry around ancestry research. You can, if you are so inclined, trace your family line back hundreds of years. I met a lady on the platform at Reading station a few weeks ago who told me she only took a train once a year, and that her annual trip was always to visit a new twig on the vast family tree she was piecing together. 'I'm not married and I don't have children,' she told me. 'It's nice to feel I'm part of something.' We might not have particularly exciting ancestors, but a connection to the past gives us grounding. It gives us context.

There are a few of my family's stories that have been particularly defining for me. My paternal grandfather left a senior position at a large engineering firm just as he was poised for a promotion that would have made us wealthy for generations, because he wasn't enjoying himself and wanted the last years of his career to count. He set up an orthopaedic engineering unit at Oxford University and pioneered some groundbreaking medical technology, some of which he was able to adapt for use in areas of the world where people face extreme poverty. My maternal great-grandmother was a hilarious eccentric, known for her acerbic wit and convention-flouting antics. She once asked her host what she should wear to an upcoming dinner. On receiving the offhand response, 'Oh nothing. Just come,' she showed up in a full-length fur coat under which she was wearing, as specified, nothing (other than some frilly underwear). My paternal great-grandfather founded a mission in the slums of East London that survives to this day. My maternal grandmother was raised in almost total isolation in rural Ireland, and yet courageously joined the Wrens at the outbreak of World War Two, the first time she'd been away from home, and her first exposure to a large group of peers. I could go on, but I'm sure your family stories are far more interesting than mine. Maybe this is a good time to dig some of them out, or go and visit the elders of your tribe and gather some more.

King David was able to trace his ancestry across thirteen generations, all the way back to Abraham. He knew his family line inside out, and we know it too, because it turned out to be the family into which Jesus was born. The people of Israel had an identity created and sustained by their stories, stories God had commanded them to pass on, telling and retelling them so that they would become part of their very DNA. Their family stories included covenants with the Almighty God, miraculous babies and dreadful floods, slavery and an escape from the Egyptian army on a dry path through the sea, heavenly food in a barren wilderness, a promised land and a coming Messiah. David's psalms and prayers are interspersed with these stories. They anchor him in a huge metanarrative.

One of the major themes running through the story of the people of Israel and the story of David's life is the search for a place to belong. The Israelites learned through long years in the desert that God was with them and would provide the essentials for survival, but God saw their need to settle somewhere safe, somewhere they could call their own. Soon after building his palace in Jerusalem, David had a visit from the prophet Nathan with this message from the Lord: 'I took you from the pasture, from tending the flock, and appointed you ruler over my people Israel. I have been with you wherever you have gone, and I have cut off all your enemies from before you. Now I will make your name like the names of the greatest men on earth. And I will provide a place for my people Israel and will plant them so that they can have a home of their own and no longer be disturbed.'[4] God had been with the Israelites, and with David in all his wandering. But God understands that people flourish when they are planted.

For Christians, these ancient stories are in some way our stories too. We worship the same God David did. We are grafted onto the roots of Israel,[5] and so our identity is shaped by biblical history as much as it is by our personal and family histories.

Toxic nostalgia

We are unique among the animals in our propensity to look back over time. It is a gift, this ability to bring the past into the present. And it can also be a curse.

It is April 2016. We walk out of Girona Airport in

northern Spain, here for a week of family holiday. The air is yellow and dusty. 'Everything looks dirty,' says Alexa. I try and see it through her eyes, but it just looks *right* to me. There are pines, rosemary bushes, olive groves. 'I just saw lemons on trees,' Charis says in surprise. I feel almost sick with a sudden intensity of feeling I have no word for. I tell them that this is quite like the place where I grew up, and take a long, deep breath, searching for the smell. I can't quite find it, and I remember how when I was a child and we drove back into Portugal from Spain the car would erupt with cheers and whoops of joy to be back on familiar territory. Spain is closer to Portugal than England though and I'm just happy to be here.

However, the sense of 'almost but not quite right' persists through the week. Hints of another place and time tease me, glint in the corner of my eye, tap me on the shoulder, only to whip out of sight. The cliffs below the hilltop town of Begur are too orange and the water is too green. The sand is made of minute shells: beautiful, yes, but not the white dust of the Algarvian beaches. We find Hottentot figs and I show the girls how to snap the fat triangular leaves and use the juice to paint on the hot, dry rocks. I'm reaching for a memory that doesn't really belong here, and I'm starting to wonder if all this hankering after the past is getting in the way of the present.

We spend our last afternoon on the beach. We're the only tourists here; the Costa Brava fills up only in late May, once good weather is guaranteed. The girls swim, while locals in quilted jackets walk their dogs briskly along the shoreline, giving us the kind of glances that make us question our parenting judgement. At the back of the beach are sand dunes, fake ones made by a digger, but good enough for a post-swim run-around to warm up. We climb to the top and run headlong down, over and over until Charis falls flat on her face. I wait for the wails, but she lifts her sand-coated head and laughs and laughs. It's a good moment. I make sure I fix it in my mind, pinning it in place like a butterfly in a display case.

When we get back home I'm unsettled. I feel antsy and distracted. I look around at the suburban streets and the disappointingly grey May skies and I want to shrug it off, step out of it like a snake shedding its skin. I've allowed myself to indulge in the notion that I belong somewhere other than here, and it takes me weeks of disciplined challenging of my thoughts and feelings to re-embrace where I am.

We had a running joke in our family when I was growing up. We could be anywhere in the world, and Mum would notice something – a smell perhaps; a particularly green field or a lone sheep – and she'd say wistfully, 'It could be Wales.' It became standard for us to draw facetious comparisons with Pembrokeshire wherever we went. But I understand her impulse now. If it was like Wales, it was like home.

There is nothing wrong with happy childhood memories. There is nothing bad about looking back and remembering times and places in which we once belonged. There is nothing wrong with recollecting the past with affection and gratitude. But we must be alert to the danger of thinking home was back then, not now. Unless we reject that notion, there will be no cure for our homesickness. We can't return to a home in the past.

The word 'nostalgia' comes from two Greek words: *nostos* meaning 'homecoming' and *algos*, 'pain'. It was coined by Johannes Hofer, a seventeenth-century scholar at the University of Basel, and it was originally used to denote severe homesickness, understood as a medical condition at the time. *The Cyclopaedia of Practical Medicine*, published in England in 1833, lists 'nostalgia' under endemic diseases, defined as 'The concourse of depressing symptoms which sometimes arise in persons who are absent from their native country, when they are seized with a longing desire of returning to their home and friends and the scenes of their youth . . .'[6] We can never return to the past. That is the brutal truth of it. We are separated by time, an impregnable barrier, and all the longing in the world cannot take us back there. If we don't shake ourselves roughly, grit our teeth, and determine to set our faces towards the rising sun, we'll grow sick with nostalgia. We'll find we are homeless.

Ecclesiastes 7:10 says, 'Do not say, "Why were the old days better than these?" For it is not wise to ask such questions.' When we have been blessed with 'golden eras' in our lives, we can be tempted to continually hark back to them. 'Nostalgia,' writes the Old Testament professor Ellen Davis about this verse, 'is essentially a repudiation of the possibility of present joy . . . loving the past cannot mean wishing ourselves back into it; that is the vanity (absurdity) of nostalgia.'[7]

Memory is not reliable, and often what we think we long for, what we believe we once had and lost forever, never even existed. We are free to idealise a past house, a friendship, a church we were once part of, the hamlet we grew up in where everyone knew each other, because who can challenge our account of how it was? If we allow ourselves to luxuriate in nostalgia, the myth of a beautiful, long-gone past will solidify, and it will weigh us down. Much as we must fight the idea that we would be happier somewhere else, in another marriage, in a bigger house, we must fight the idea that we were once at home but we never will be again.

One of Saint Benedict's monastic vows was the vow of stability, committing those who took it to seek God *in this place.* While the vow was geographical in its intended scope, it could just as easily be applied in a temporal sense. Philip Sheldrake writes, 'The desert tradition of monastic life placed a central emphasis on the importance of staying in one place, specifically the "cell", in order to find God. The point was stressed that if one could not find God in stability, there was no guarantee that God could be experienced by moving anywhere else. Stability in itself was also a protection against seeking to assuage spiritual boredom by wandering hither and thither.'[8] In the same way, we must make home now, or we won't find it in the future, and must face the fact that quite possibly we didn't have it in the past.

Humans are story-telling, story-dwelling creatures. We

are created with an instinct for narrative, and our narratives are what transform places and people into home. Find your story, tell it and live it, and it will show you where you belong.

Where is home?

ON 29 OCTOBER 2001, the Right Reverend David Rea Cochran, retired bishop of Alaska, brought the last chapter of his memoirs, which he had titled *Going Home*, into the office of St Matthew's Church in Tacoma, Washington, for proof-reading. A local church newspaper reported that 'Less than 24 hours later Bishop Cochran, 86, had himself gone home', having died quietly in his sleep.

When I've told Christians that I'm thinking and writing about the meaning of home, many of them have nodded knowingly and said something along the lines of, 'Ah yes – of course, heaven is our real home.' I think heaven looms large in thoughts about home because for believers it is often the only thing that makes sense of suffering and that persistent sense that they don't quite belong. African slaves in the United States sang a lot of songs about heaven, expressing deep yearning for this eternal home where they would be free and safe. This week I heard the story of an Iranian given a death sentence for his faith, who told the court at his final hearing that he was not afraid to die because he knew where he was going.

Over the last meal Jesus shared with his followers before his crucifixion, he talked about his Father's house, where there was plenty of room for all of them. The Bible doesn't give detailed specifics about what awaits beyond the grave, but the picture we have is of a renewed earth where, as in Eden, God lives among his people. There will be no pain, no tears, no displacement or loneliness. There will be no exile or separation; no earthquakes or landslides destroying houses; no bereavement, no redundancies, firings or unemployment; no culture shock, no language barriers, no homesickness. Our search for a place to belong will be over.

If you don't believe in God or life after death, you'll find that sentiment a bit empty, and although I'm a Christian I reject the notion that we cannot be truly at home until we die. We are never going to achieve permanence, because our universe is on the move through space and time and nothing stays the same, but we *can* be at home here and now, despite the knowledge it won't be our home for ever – in fact, all the more so because heaven will be the completion of all the good that home brings us.

Home is the place where we live, be it a house, an

apartment, a caravan or a rented room. Home is among the people who love us, our families, our friends, our church, our community. Home is our culture, the language we speak, the food we eat, the books we read and the jokes we find funny. Home is our country, the landscapes and weather systems and the architecture. Home is within ourselves. Home is where we belong, the place we come back to.

Home is the end of our quest.

Book Group Questions

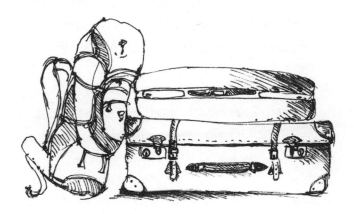

1. Has your understanding of what or where home is changed as you've read the book? If so, how?

2. The philosopher Simone Weil believed that 'to be rooted is perhaps the most important and least recognised needs of the human soul'. What does it mean to have roots? Where are your roots planted?

3. What has been your experience of homesickness?

4. What did the idea of home mean to the biblical character David? How did his relationship with God shape his attitude towards the places and people he encountered through his life?

5. In what ways can we offer home to those in need of a place to belong?

6. Is your tendency towards staying in one place or constantly moving on? How might each attitude be seen as the good and godly way to live? And what might make each spiritually disobedient?

7. Of all the facets that make up a sense of home, what is the one that resonates with you the most? Is your home primarily your house, your neighbourhood, your family, your church, your country? Why?

8. How can we have a strong connection to our past without indulging in nostalgia? Why can nostalgia be toxic?

9. What makes a house a home?

10. How do you picture heaven? How can we make our home here and now, while also living in the hopeful expectation of a permanent, eternal home?

Acknowledgements

Of all the words that have gone into this book, these are the hardest to find. The task of adequately thanking those who have invested in me and this piece of writing is daunting, to say the least. I'm sitting here quite overcome with gratitude. I'd like to acknowledge and thank the following people:

My parents, for being my first home and for making everywhere they've lived a place of belonging for anyone who comes through the door. My mum worked diligently on my first draft and her edits raised the standard of my writing beyond all recognition.

My team of first readers who gave me early critique and encouragement: Sarah Lothian, Julia Ovchinnikova, Sheridan Voysey, David Lindsell and Esther Youlten.

Ian Metcalfe at Hodder, for skilled editing, insightful questions and an implicit understanding of the heart of what I wanted to say.

The staff at Ex Cellar in Surbiton, especially Lisa, Crystal and Kathryn, for keeping the Americanos with hot skimmed milk coming, for cheering me on and for letting me treat the place like I owned it.

Charlie and Anita Cleverly, for giving me a writing home

away from home and for believing I have something to say.

All those who let me tell their stories, especially Erika, Justin, Sarah, Sophie, Martin and Gary.

Eugene Peterson, one of my all-time favourite authors. Among his many books, all of which are worth more than their weight in platinum (see how I sidestepped a tired phrase there?), is a wonderful weaving together of David stories and reflections on the Christian life, called *Leap Over a Wall: Earthy Spirituality for Everyday Christians*. I'm deeply indebted and unashamedly influenced by this book, and heartily recommend you read it just as soon as you've finished this one.

Shawn, Alexa and Charis, for giving me time and space to write over these busy months, for keeping me sane with your love and your silliness and for making my life better than I could ever have imagined.

Notes

1 The Portuguese phrase translates as, 'Wherever you are, I am at home.'

Prologue

1 Maslow amended the model to include self-transcendence in 1969.

Chapter Two

1 See John Bowlby, 'Attachment theory and its therapeutic implications', *Adolescent Psychiatry*, vol. 6, 5–33 (1978).
2 Christopher Lasch, *Haven in a Heartless World* (New York: Basic Books, 1977), p. 3.
3 The colloquial name for the Royal Canadian Mounted Police.
4 Rough paraphrase of 1 Samuel 17:28.
5 Actual quote of David, 1 Samuel 17:29.
6 1 Samuel 16:13.
7 Luke 8:21.
8 Romans 8:14, 16.
9 Donald Miller and John MacMurray, *To Own a Dragon* (Carol Stream, IL: Navpress, 2006). It was later republished as *Father Fiction: Chapters for a Fatherless Generation* (London: Hodder and Stoughton, 2010).
10 *To Own a Dragon*, p. 69.
11 Ibid., p. 186.

12 Rodney Clapp, *Families at the Crossroads* (Westmont, IL: InterVarsity Press, 1993), p. 67.

Chapter Three

1   In case you are wondering, it is pronounced *Mesh-loo-ay-ra Grande.*
2   For a history of this field of research, see http://www.tckworld.com/useem/art1.html
3   Norma M. McCaig, 'Growing Up with a World View: Nomad Children Develop Multicultural Skills', *Foreign Service Journal*, September 1994, pp. 32–41.
4   Heidi Sand-Hart, *Home Keeps Moving: A Glimpse into the Extraordinary Life of a Third Culture Kid* (Hagerstown, MD: McDougal Publishing, 2010).
5   Ibid., p. 21.
6   Thirdculturekid.blogspot.com
7   See John 15:19, John 17:14, James 1:27, 1 John 2:15.
8   You can read more of how this happened in Genesis 11:1–9.
9   Leviticus 13:49–50.
10 Eugene Peterson, *The Message: The Bible in Contemporary Language* (Carol Stream, IL: NavPress, 1993), Romans 12:1–2.
11 I find this little detail quite hilarious! See 1 Samuel 10:20–23.
12 1 Samuel 18:2.
13 From Psalm 69.

Chapter Four

1   A *fado* is a type of popular Portuguese song, usually with a melancholy theme and accompanied by mandolins or guitars.
2   1 Samuel 27.
3   Joshua 3:1–3.
4   For Brueggemann's full argument, see Walter Brueggemann,

The Land: Place as Gift, Promise, and Challenge in Biblical Faith (Minneapolis, MN: Fortress Press, 1977).

5 Translation of French and Arabic lyrics from www.nation-alanthems.info

6 And now, as I finalise the manuscript, we do. God bless America.

7 Jeremiah 29:5–7.

8 Acts 17:26–27.

9 Hebrews 11:13, 16.

Chapter Five

1 Peter Harris, *Kingfisher's Fire* (Oxford: Monarch Books, 2008), p. 46.

2 Evagrius Ponticus, *The Praktikos & Chapters on Prayer.* Trans. John Eudes Bamberger (Collegeville, MN: Cistercian Publications, 1981), pp. 18–19.

3 Kathleen Norris, *Acedia & Me: A Marriage, Monks, and a Writer's Life* (New York: Riverhead Books, 2008), p. 25.

4 Philippians 4:12.

5 *No Place to Call Home*, produced and directed by Luke Sewell, first aired on BBC2 on 18 October 2016.

6 Psalm 34:9.

7 Psalm 57:7.

8 Psalm 63:3.

Chapter Six

1 The title of a book written by Theresa of Avila in 1577.

2 I wrote about my depression in my first book, *Through the Dark Woods* (Oxford: Monarch Books, 2006).

3 Psalm 139:11–12.

4 https://www.ted.com/talks/brene_brown_on_vulnerability, accessed 20 November 2016.

5 Paula Gooder, *Body: Biblical spirituality for the whole person* (London: SPCK, 2016), p. 16.

Chapter Seven

1 Mike Mason, *The Mystery of Marriage* (Colorado Springs, CO: Multnomah Press, 1985), p. 219.
2 Created by Moving Works Films. Available at https://movingworks.org/project/chloe
3 Song of Songs 8:6–7.
4 1 Samuel 18:21.
5 1 Samuel 25:30–31.
6 1 Samuel 25:3.
7 Try saying Ish-Bosheth after a couple of pints . . .
8 Eugene Peterson, *Leap Over a Wall: Reflections on the Life of David* (San Francisco: HarperCollins, 1998), p. 189.
9 Sheldon Vanauken, *A Severe Mercy: C. S. Lewis's influence on a moving and tragic love story* (London: Hodder and Stoughton, 2011).
10 Mike Mason, *The Mystery of Marriage: Meditations on the Miracle* (Colorado Springs, CO: Multnomah Press, 1985), p. 44.

Chapter Eight

1 Brueggemann, *The Land*, p. 5.
2 http://denizenmag.com/2013/10/the-real-challenge-was-to-stay, accessed on 16 July 2016.
3 Christopher Tilley, *Metaphor and Material Culture* (Oxford: Blackwell Publishers, 1999), p. 177.
4 Loren and Mary Ruth Wilkinson, *Caring for Creation in your own Backyard* (Vancouver: Regent College Publishing, 1992), p. 207.
5 https://www.ted.com/talks/marwa_al_sabouni_how_syria_s_architecture_laid_the_foundation_for_brutal_war, accessed 10 November 2016.
6 Psalm 122:2–9.
7 Peterson, *Leap Over a Wall*, p. 133.
8 Luke 19:43–44.

9   See Romans 8 for starters. Then I would highly recommend
     N. T. Wright, *New Heavens, New Earth: The Biblical Picture
     of Christian Hope* (Cambridge: Grove Books, 1999) as a
     great introduction.

Chapter Nine

1   Bill Bryson, *At Home: A Short History of Private Life*
     (London: Transworld Publishers, 2010), p. 55.
2   http://www.interiordesign.net/articles/11310-design-fore-
     cast-10-trends-to-watch-for-in-2016, accessed 9 December
     2016.
3   Reported in *The Mirror*, 2 September 2015.
4   See for example http://www.bbc.co.uk/news/world-latin-
     america-37596222
5   1 Chronicles 11:9.
6   1 Chronicles 14:2.

Chapter Ten

1   Kennon L. Callahan, *Effective Church Leadership* (San
     Francisco: Harper, 1990), p. 102.
2   John 13:34–35.
3   John 14:23.
4   Jean Vanier, *Community and Growth* (Mahwah, NJ: Paulist
     Press, 1989), p. 63.
5   You can read about this incident in 2 Samuel 6 and
     1 Chronicles 13.
6   1 Corinthians 3:16.

Chapter Eleven

1   Frederick Buechner, *Wishful Thinking: A Seeker's ABC* (San
     Francisco: HarperCollins, 1993), p. 119.
2   Parker J. Palmer, *Let Your Life Speak: Listening for the
     Voice of Vocation* (San Francisco: Jossey-Bass, 2000), p. 15.

3   Annie Dillard, *The Writing Life* (New York: HarperCollins, 1989), p. 32.

Chapter Twelve

1   Lewis J. Crawford, *The Exploits of Ben Arnold: Indian Fighter, Gold Miner, Cowboy, Hunter, & Army Scout* (Oklahoma: The University of Oklahoma Press, 2000).

2   Brené Brown, *Rising Strong* (London: Penguin Random House, 2015), p. 249.

3   Bruce Feiler, 'The Stories that Bind Us', *The New York Times* (15 March 2013).

4   1 Chronicles 17:7–9.

5   Romans 11:11–24.

6   Cited on http://www.etymonline.com/index.php?term=nostalgia, accessed 7 October 2016.

7   Ellen F. Davis, *Proverbs, Ecclesiastes, and the Song of Songs* (Louisville, KY: Westminster John Knox Press, 2000), pp. 201–02.

8   Philip Sheldrake, *Spaces for the Sacred: Place, Memory, and Identity* (Baltimore, MD: The Johns Hopkins University Press, 2001), p. 109.